BLUES-BY YOU

The Direct Route To Piano Improvisation

by Joel Simpson

Edited by Ronny Schiff

This book is dedicated to Henry Butler, teacher, artist, and friend. I would like to thank Robert Laughlin of the New School for American Music in Paradise, California, for the inspiration to create this book, and Ronny Schiff for her excellent editing suggestions.

Copyright © 1997 Cherry Lane Music Company
International Copyright Secured
All Rights Reserved

The music, text, design and graphics in this publication are
protected by copyright law. Any duplication or transmission,
by any means, electronic, mechanical, photocopying,
recording or otherwise, is an infringement of copyright.

Excerpts on pages 4, 24, 26 and 49
Copyright © 1990 Stephen Nachmanovitch.
Reprinted by permission of Jeremy P. Tarcher, Inc., a division of The Putnam Publishing Group
from *Free Play* by Stephen Nachmanovitch.
International Copyright Secured All Rights Reserved

 Visit our website at www.cherrylane.com

Contents

4 **Introduction**

8 **Chapter 1**
The Basic Structure Of The Blues

12 **Chapter 2**
Blues Rhythm

16 **Chapter 3**
Melodic Embellishments

20 **Chapter 4**
Creating Your Own Blues Riffs

24 **Interlude**
The Deep Structure Of The Blues

26 **Chapter 5**
The Blues Melodic Line I:
A Subtractive Approach

32 **Chapter 6**
The Blues Melodic Line II:
An Additive Approach

39 **Chapter 7**
Speaking The Blues Language

45 **Chapter 8**
Adding Variety

49 **Coda**

51 **Suggested Reading**

Editor's Note

• Unless otherwise noted, the music in this book is to be played with a swing feel in which a pair of eighth notes that begin on the beat are executed as the first two-thirds and last third of an eighth-note triplet.

• All examples are in 4 time.

INTRODUCTION

As an improvising musician, I am not in the music business, I am not in the creativity business; I am in the surrender business.

—Stephen Nachmanovitch *Free Play,*

You Can Play Blues And Boogie-Woogie Piano!

The blues is one of the most popular, widespread, influential, and expressive styles of music. Perhaps what is best about it is that you can learn it in a series of relatively simple steps. If you take one step at a time and master it thoroughly, you can be playing a good-sounding blues solo in an astonishingly short time—usually in about a month or two, with 30 to 60 minutes of practice each day. In another couple of months, at the same rate, you should be producing interesting improvisations.

Learning the blues offers a direct route to piano improvisation. Don't let the idea of improvising scare you. Remember, you do it every time you talk—and you do it in rhythm too! If you are a schooled pianist, trained to read notes and memorize music, remember that before you took your first lesson you were probably improvising at the keyboard, you just didn't know the rules.

The blues uses a relatively small number of rules (jazz uses many more) and a minimum of music theory. Yet these few rules are so well constructed that they lend themselves to an infinite number of possibilities, and inspire a whole universe of variations and emotional expression.

When you learn the blues, you learn a musical language spoken all over the world. You will be able to play with other musicians and experience the fun and deep satisfaction of purely musical communication.

The Joy Of Playing The Blues

The blues is more than a series of notes over a chord progression. Playing the blues—*saying something* with the blues—involves more than just randomly exploring the blues scale or mixing and matching patterns. It involves understanding the meaning and the power in the blues structure and the blues scale: the ability to get inside the tones of the music, so that even just a single note is filled with meaning. It also involves the patience to listen to yourself inwardly, to wait for an idea or a feeling before playing it.

By listening to *and* playing each of the musical examples in this book, you will absorb—layer by layer—a multitude of blues techniques, and develop a rich blues style. When you finish the book you will also be ready to branch out into any of the rich musical traditions nourished by the blues, such as R&B, jazz, gospel, and rock. Your understanding of the blues that you hear in performance and on recordings will deepen, and you will be able to quickly assimilate the ideas you hear with increasing ease. As you keep listening and playing, the broad range of blues expressiveness will become clearer. You will find that playing the blues can be a meditation, a joyous invitation, an exultation, a lament, a scream of protest, a dejected whisper, or simply an engaging monologue or conversation.

Prerequisites

This book is aimed at people who have had some keyboard background. If you are a rank beginner, you should take an introductory keyboard course at a local college or university (try their extension division), or find a private teacher. If you do have some keyboard background, this book will take you from a beginning to a solid intermediate level in solo blues and boogie-woogie piano.

The CD And Beyond

The CD that comes with this book presents all the musical examples. Listen to each example, then play it yourself, slowly at first (hands separately if you need to). When you have an example up to speed, play along with the recording to capture the nuances. Make sure you have mastered each example before going on to the next one, but don't restrict yourself to the literal examples. Each one is meant to broaden your blues vocabulary. Explore. Go back over previous examples and combine new material with old to come up with fresh ideas. There are many suggestions how to do so throughout this book.

Using A Metronome

Use a metronome. Some metronome markings are included as guides to tempo. Remember that the same music can have different meanings when played at different tempos. Your intuition or gut feeling will tell you this. Listen to it. If something seems too complicated, then break it down, isolating the part that gives you trouble and practice that part slowly. (See "How To Learn Anything Using A Metronome" on page 14.) When playing with the metronome, try setting it to tick once every two beats. Then "place" the ticks on the back beats, beats 2 and 4. This will simulate a drummer's hi-hat, and help develop your sense of groove.

How To Practice

1. Keep a small notebook of lined paper (not music paper) at your keyboard.
2. Write the date and the time you sit down to begin your session. Write the time you finish or interrupt yourself and when you sit back down.
3. Make a list of the projects (examples, pieces, etc.) you intend to work on that day. This should be realistic and reflect the amount of time you intend to spend at the keyboard.
4. Each project should have a specific goal, which includes a goal *tempo*. Write down your starting tempo for that day and the tempo you reach.
5. Each day's practice should include some time for free exploratory play: try what you are doing from a new perspective, invent something, attempt to play something you have heard. If you are comfortable reading music, play some sheet music and see how you can make it your own. Try to practice an hour a day. Remember that several short sessions in a day can be more effective than a single long one.

The Importance Of Listening

The blues is an aurally transmitted music. Of course, much of this music has been transcribed and printed in books, but listening is of *critical* importance. Certain vitally important elements are *never* represented on the page. They are learned by being heard and imitated. The difference between a good player and a great player often lies in just these very elements that are not written down.

Here are some key questions you can ask yourself when listening to music:

- How does this music work?
- What is its attraction?
- How does it hold the listener's attention?
- What elements are changing or evolving?
- What are the dramatic elements or devices?
- What are its most powerful emotional elements?

Suggested Listening

Even though the guitar and voice have tended to predominate the blues, the blues piano tradition is a strong one, dating to the early years of the 20th century. Blues piano/keyboard players fall into four general categories, with some overlap:

Blues Roots Pianists

Jimmy Yancey, Champion Jack Dupree, Little Brother Montgomery, Speckled Red, Roosevelt Sykes, Otis Spann, Memphis Slim, Alex Moore, Kid Stormy Weather, Cow-Cow Davenport, "Jelly Roll" Morton, Meade Lux Lewis, Albert Ammons, Dink Johnson, and Sunnyland Slim (see the *Bibliography* for transcriptions).

Jazz-Oriented Blues Pianists

Ray Bryant, Les McCann, Mary Lou Williams, Count Basie, Junior Mance, Mose Allison, and Charles Brown. (Every jazz pianist plays blues seriously; listen to Dave McKenna, for example.)

New Orleans–Style Pianists (R&B)

Dr. John (Mac Rebennack), Professor Longhair (Henry Roeland Byrd), James Booker, and Henry Butler. There is a heavy gospel influence here as well as Latin and funk.

Contemporary Blues/Funk Players

Stevie Wonder, Herbie Hancock, Billy Preston, Ramsey Lewis, Charles Earland, Steve Winwood, Richard Tee, Joey DeFrancesco and Kankawa; the bands of James Brown, Tower of Power, Earth Wind and Fire, Roomful of Blues; also organists Jimmy Smith, and Jimmy McGriff.

Of course, listen to blues being played live! Find clubs in your area where the blues is played, or go to jazz clubs and request the blues. Musicians generally love to be asked to play the blues.

Chapter 1

The Basic Structure Of The Blues

The 12-Bar Blues

The blues has appeared in many forms. The most common is the 12-bar blues, but there are also 8-bar and 16-bar blueses. The 12-bar blues stabilized in the 1920s, although many barrelhouse* pianists continued to play a blues of indeterminate form.

The 12-bar blues has a number of different chord pattern possibilities. You will be using the following, perhaps most common, one as your foundation (there will be some variations later). It is shown here in the key of C.

How To Play Ex. 1

- Tap your foot (four beats to a bar).
- Play with the left hand only, coming down on the first beat of each bar.
- Hold each chord for the entire bar.

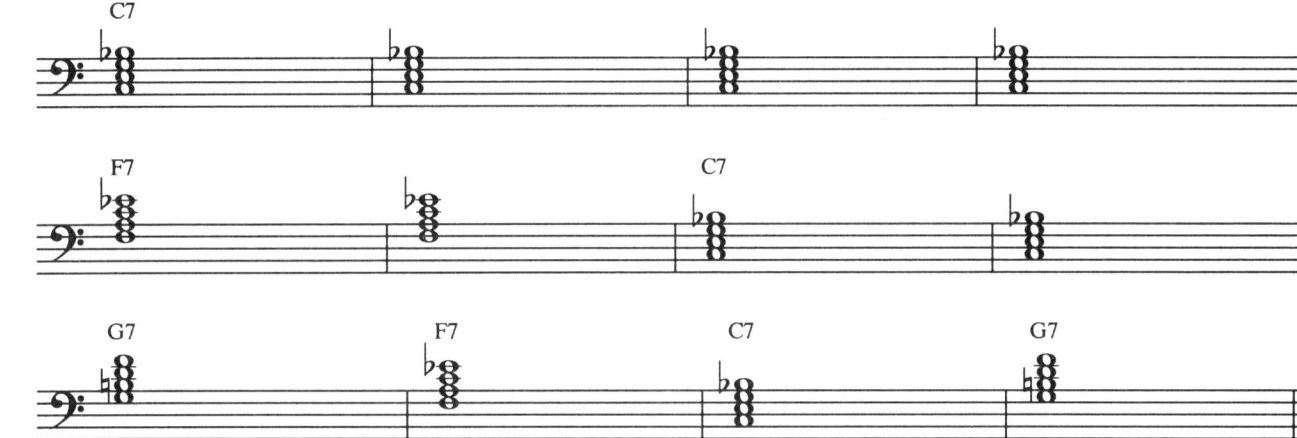

The 12-bar blues contains three four-bar phrases. When sung, each four-bar section contains one line or sentence. The first line (bars 1–4) is repeated in the second (bars 5–8), and then a response is given in the last line (bars 9–12). Keep this simple structure in mind to give your blues form and meaning.

The last bar is called the *turnaround*. It prepares the listener for the 12-bar blues form to start over at the beginning again–repeatedly.

---

*An improvisatory blues piano style that developed in the rural dance halls of the South (frequented entirely by African-Americans) from about 1910 through the 1940s. Some barrelhouse pianists, including Sunnyland Slim, Blind Lemon Jefferson, and Cow-Cow Davenport, made recordings.

Chords Have Different Names

In addition to the letter-based names, such as C7, F7, or B♭7♯11, chords have names according to their harmonic function. These functional names are useful because *they are the same in whatever key you are playing*, whereas the letter-based names change every time you change the key.

The principal chord of a piece, the one built on the 1st scale degree of the key, is called the *I chord* or *tonic chord*. Thus, C is the tonic in the key of C; A♭ is the tonic in the key of A♭, and so on.

The chord built on the 5th scale degree is called the *V chord* or the *dominant*. In C, it is G; in F, it is C; in A♭, it is E♭; and so on. The chord built on the 4th scale degree is called the *IV chord* or the *subdominant*. In C, it is F; in F, it is B♭; in A♭, it is D♭; and so on. These will be the main chords with which you will be dealing in this book. Blues and jazz players tend to refer to chord functions by the Roman numerals (spoken as "the five chord," "the one chord"), rather than using the words *dominant* or *subdominant*.

Range And Register

You will notice that, in this book, the lowest note played as part of a chord is the C below middle C. Chords played lower than that tend to sound muddy, but played in the right register they will sound clear and strong—not muddy—and interfere as little as possible with the right hand.

An Easier Way: Inversions

The chords in Ex. 1 are in *root position*, with the root, or letter name, of the chord on the bottom. When chords are voiced this way they are easy to find and to spell, but they are not in the easiest position to play. Your hand has to jump up four notes to move from C7 to F7, and even farther to the G7 chord.

An easier (and better-sounding) way to play these chords is to use *inversions*. An inversion is created by using a chord tone other than the root as the lowest note of the voicing. A seventh chord, which contains four notes, has a root position plus three inversions, making four possible versions of the chord.

A Blues Chorus With Inversions

The chords in this example are the same as those in Ex. 1, but here the C7 chord is played in *second inversion*, that is, with the 5th in the bass. The sound of the progression is much smoother now, due to the closeness of the notes between the different chords. If inversions are new to you, practice alternating root position and second inversion for each of the chords.

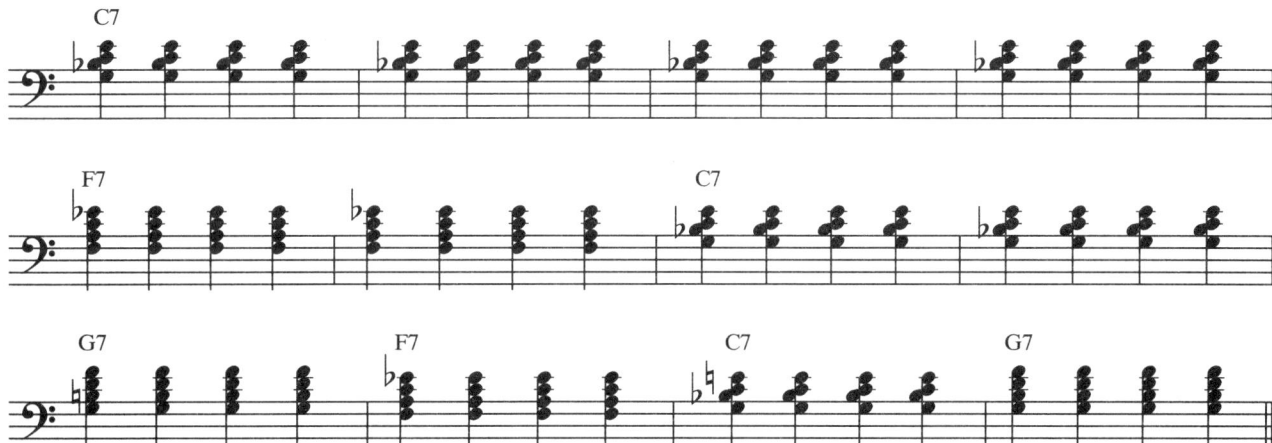

Supplementary Exercise For Beginners

If you are having trouble moving from chord-to-chord—hesitating or stumbling, breaking the flow of the rhythm—practice changing adjacent chords. That is, play C7 and F7 in alternation, first slowly, accurately, then pick up the speed. Do the same with the C7–G7 transition and the G7–F7. When you put it all back together it should flow smoothly.

If you are still having problems, break it down into even simpler terms. The following exercise works like magic, because it teaches each finger its role in the chord change separately and then in combination with each other finger. To move between the root position C7 and F7 in the left hand with a 1-2-3-5 fingering,

1. *Play only the notes the thumb plays, back and forth: B♭–E♭–B♭–E♭–etc.–ten times. Then play only the notes the second finger plays: G–C–G–C–etc.–ten times. Then do the same for the 3rd and 5th fingers.*
2. *Play all possible combinations of two notes: G and B♭ to C and E♭ and back; E and G to A and C and back; C and E to F and A and back; then E and B♭ to A and E♭ and back; C and G to F and C and back; C and B♭ to F and E♭ and back; get the idea?*
3. *Play all possible combinations of three notes.*
4. *When you get ready to play all four notes they should just fall into place.*
5. *Do the same thing with the right hand until you are fluent with it, then play Ex. 1, hands together, two octaves apart.*

This exercise will work for any two adjacent chords in any inversion or voicing. You can also use it when practicing successive inversions of the same chord. Simply find the precise moment of chord transition, then analyze what each finger (or pair of adjacent fingers) does.

Intervals

Intervals are to music what syllables are to language. They are the smallest units of musical meaning, and they are defined by the *distance between two notes*. The octave contains twelve different intervals, each with a distinct sound and name. A mastery of the sounds of intervals and how they combine gives you a powerful tool to create music.

Once you understand the names of the intervals and begin to recognize their sounds it will be easier to understand what makes up the sound of the blues and how to create the strongest effects when playing the blues.

Illustration 1

Find the intervals shown above on your keyboard. Play them and listen to them. Notice the following things about them:

- Each one may be broken down into a certain number of half steps (the smallest possible unit on the keyboard).

minor 2nd	= 1 half step	[C–D♭]
major 2nd	= 2 half steps (a whole step)	[C–D]
minor 3rd	= 3 half steps	[C–E♭]
major 3rd	= 4 half steps (2 whole steps)	[C–E]
perfect 4th	= 5 half steps	[C–F]
diminished 5th	= 6 half steps (3 whole steps)	[C–G♭]
perfect 5th	= 7 half steps	[C–G]
minor 6th	= 8 half steps (4 whole steps)	[C–A♭]
major 6th	= 9 half steps	[C–A]
minor 7th	= 10 half steps (5 whole steps)	[C–B♭]
major 7th	= 11 half steps	[C–B]
octave	= 12 half steps (6 whole steps)	[C–C]

- The names and the sizes (distances) of the intervals remain the same no matter on which note they start. Illustration 1 could have been printed 12 times starting on 12 different notes.
- If you play the bottom note of an interval an octave higher, you'll get the interval's *inversion*, which is different for each interval, except the diminished 5th (or *tritone*). (If you do this for the octave you get a unison.)
- The sum of the half-steps contained in any interval and its inversion is always 12.

Each interval has a characteristic sound. These sounds are the building blocks of music in the same way that syllables (or technically, *phonemes*) are the building blocks of language. The blues favors certain intervallic sounds, and you will come to recognize them.

Blues Rhythm

The Immediacy Of Rhythm
Of all the basic elements of music—melody, harmony, rhythm and timbre—rhythm is the one to which people relate most immediately and most basically. In this sense it is the most important element. The blues is fundamentally a dance form, for which rhythm is indispensable. Rhythm speaks directly to the listener's body, that makes him want to move. This is what you're after: rhythms that motivate.

The Charleston Rhythm
With all the rhythmic variety in the blues, there are two basic rhythmic concepts that are essential The first is the Charleston, or "hambone," rhythm (♪ ♩ ♪ ♩). This example shows the Charleston rhythm in the right hand over quarter-note chords in the left.

Triplet Rhythm
The second fundamental rhythmic pattern is the "broken triplet" (the middle note of the triplet is not played). This is the most common rhythm of the left-hand boogie-woogie pattern, but it is also used extensively in right-hand playing. This is also referred to as "swing" rhythm. Sometimes the music should be played with straight eighth notes, giving it different feel. In these cases, if the music is written out it will always indicate "straight eighths," since this is the less common interpretation.

Reading up from the bottom, this two-note "chord" consists of the root and 5th alternating with the root and 6th. Can you play this pattern based on F? on G?

Illustration 2

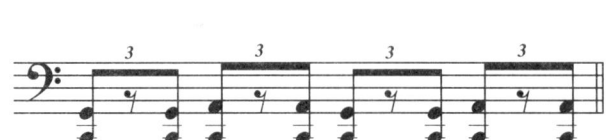

Here is an entire boogie-woogie left-hand part. Observe the fingering of $\frac{2}{5}$ to $\frac{1}{5}$. Learn this fingering now and it will serve you well at quicker tempos. Practice this example until you can play it smoothly at a fast tempo, and, of course, memorize it. This is the boogie-blues foundation. It can be played from ♩=80 to ♩=200.

Putting The Hands Together

This blues in C combines the right-hand Charleston rhythm with the left-hand boogie-woogie pattern. It is better if you can figure this out for yourself without reading it. If you need to check on what you are playing, go ahead, but learn this by heart, and play it until it makes sense to you. Remember: When you put your hands together, play slower than you practiced either hand separately.

Notice that the right-hand rhythm changes slightly in the last bar, creating a dramatic end for the chorus, and "resetting" the ear for the next chorus.

How To Learn Anything Using A Metronome

A metronome is an essential tool for any musician. Most music stores sell the nine-volt-battery-operated kind for around $35. Once you have one, you can learn to play music that appears difficult by following these steps:

1. *Choose the first manageable section of the music.*
   This may be the right hand or left hand of a single bar, a single phrase, or an entire page.

2. *Find the tempo on your metronome at which you can play the passage perfectly, and at which you are relaxed playing it.*
   If you are playing it perfectly but feel tension in any part of your body, then you will not be able to increase the speed. Also, you will communicate that tension to your listeners. Slow down until you feel completely relaxed.

3. *Play it 20 times at that tempo.*

4. *Advance your metronome one notch and play the passage one or two times.*

5. *Continue advancing, playing the passage one to five times, and increasing the tempo until you begin to make mistakes.*

6. *Take a short or long break (or come back the next day). Then push back your metronome two notches and play the passage 10-20 times.*

7. *Repeat steps 4-6 until you have it up to the correct tempo.*

8. *Go on to the next section.*

Note: When putting passages together—either stringing them together one after the other or playing both hands together—you must start much slower than the tempo you achieved with single sections. The procedure for increasing speed is the same; however, you won't have to go all the way back to your beginning speed.

If you begin to tire of a passage, stop. Come back later or the next day. Your skill in playing a particular passage consolidates itself when you are away from your instrument—as long as you reinforce your gains on a daily basis.

Leaving Space For Greater Effectiveness

A great way to make your music more effective is by using simple yet invigorating rhythmic ideas, like in these chordal choruses. Note that only Ex. 6a is shown as a complete chorus. Exs. 6b–6e are played in truncated, four-bar versions for demonstration purposes only; you should play them as complete choruses.

Supplementary Exercise For Beginners

If you have trouble playing chords with the Charleston rhythm, try playing a full chorus of them against the left-hand chords (as in Ex. 3—one chord per beat). Look closely at the rhythm in Ex. 5. Notice that the chords fall on the first beat and between the second and third beats, on the "and" of two (**1**–&–**2**–&–**3**–&–**4**–&).

Here is the exercise: Play the left-hand chords from Ex. 2 while counting (**1**–&–**2**–&–**3**–&–**4**–&). Then you will be able to play the right-hand chords in the Charleston rhythm—on **1** and on **2&**. Therefore, on the first beat of every bar both hands will play together, but then the right hand will play its second chord exactly between the second and third chords of the left hand.

Start slowly and work up to about ♩=120. When you can do all of this easily, you will be ready to learn the boogie bass and use it instead of playing quarter-note chords with the left hand.

Melodic Embellishments

The blues is a language with idioms and familiar phrases that give the audience a feeling of reassurance. The blues contains subtle nuances that communicate certain feelings; these often minute gestures—a guitarist's or vocalist's bent note, a pianist's slide—communicate authenticity. While relatively easy to learn, these nuances can make all the difference in your playing. Ex. 7 (on the following page) adds embellishments to the chords from Ex. 5 to make you sound like more of a native speaker.

Blue Notes

One of the characteristic sounds of the blues comes from the blurring of the absolute distinction between major and minor chords. The chords used in the blues can have a major *and* minor sound at the same time; in fact, one of the most characteristic blues sounds is the regular alternation between the minor 3rd and major 3rd in a chord. In practical terms, the use of *blue notes*—in particular the ♭3 in a melody line above a major chord (1 3 5)—expresses this major/minor duality. (Note: *True* blue notes are microtonal inflections on the ♭3rd and ♭7th degrees—both of which are played slightly sharp. They can be heard in the playing of the great blues guitarists, vocalists, and horn players. Pianists simulate this sound with slides between the ♭3 and ♮3.)

How To Play A Blues Slide

There are two types of blues slides: slides to a single note and slides to a chord. While slides to a single note (see Ex. 7g) are played before the target note as grace notes, slides to a chord (see Ex. 7a–7f) should be played as *crushed* grace notes. In other words, play the grace note or notes *with* the chord, a little before the beat, then slide the grace note to its resolution while still holding the chord. This changes a dissonant chord into a consonant one. It is the pianistic equivalent of bending a note on a guitar or horn. When playing fast, it is hard to tell whether the grace note sounds by itself (before the chord), or with the chord (followed by its resolution).

In Ex. 7, slides are applied to the C7, F7, and G7 chords in several typically bluesy ways:

- 7a. Sliding from the ♭3rd to the ♮3rd of each chord.
- 7b. Sliding from G♭ to G. The G functions differently over each chord: It is the 5th of the C7, 9th of the F7, and root of the G7.
- 7c. Sliding from the ♭3 and ♭5 to the ♮3 and ♮5.
- 7d. Sliding into double-stop 3rds and 6ths—a leaner version of 7a.
- 7e. Sliding into double-stop 4ths and 5ths—a leaner version of 7b.
- 7f. Sliding E♭ to E *and* G♭ to G on the C7 chord, as in 7c. But here you have to find something new to do on the F7 and G7 chords: the arrangement of the black and white keys on the piano doesn't permit the pattern to be applied to the F7 or G7.
- 7g. One-, two-, and three-note slides to a single note.

Basic Blues Principle: Less Is More

Exs. 7d–f illustrate a basic principle of the blues: *less is more*. By taking away notes (whether they are notes of a chord or of a melody) you create a different *shape*—often a better-defined shape, one that will have more power over the listener. In this way, 4ths, 5ths, or 6ths can often sound better than the full four-note chord. You can use the omitted notes as a simple, fill-in melody.

The other application of this principle is that you can create a great deal of variety with relatively little means. Exs. 7a–7f are all variations on Ex. 5, but they take it a step further. By looking more deeply into blues phrases, you will discover how to expand them and make richer use of them. You will also see how useful it is to be able to create a series of small variations on a single phrase, device, or pattern. This principle has the added attraction of making your blues more accessible to your listeners, easier to comprehend, with a smooth development.

Applications In Full Blues Choruses

Ex. 8 is a blues that uses the same hand positions (until the very end) as Ex. 7, with the addition of a variety of easy devices:

- The thumb performs a blues slide going from E♭ to E, the ♭3rd to the ♮3rd. This known as a *false fingering*, because the same finger is used to play two adjacent notes. It is very common in the blues.

- The first F7 chord actually occurs as the end of bar 4, *anticipating* the chord change in bar 5. This is very common in blues and jazz, and gives the line forward motion, pulling it towards the next event, while the bass line stays constant, as an anchor. This asymmetry creates tension between the melody and accompaniment, or between the right and left hands, which gives life to the music.

- The melody undergoes a subtle variation in bars 5–6 that adds interest and keeps the listener's attention, while introducing no new material. Remember: *less is more*.

- The descending line in bar 11 gives you a preview of the C pentatonic minor scale (C E♭ F G B♭) (explained in Chapter 4). Notice how satisfying it feels to hear this shape after the repeated patterns that dominate the rest of the chorus.

- The C in bar 12 is dissonant over the G7 chord, but this is a characteristic sound of the blues.

Start slowly and work this example up to ♩=92.

A High-Energy Blues Chorus

The following blues chorus uses many devices you already know. The right hand plays chords in a triplet rhythm against the left hand's boogie bass pattern you have been playing all along. Like Ex. 8, this blues uses a repeating pattern over the three four-bar sections. This makes it a *riff blues*, a common variety, made popular by Count Basie's big band in the 1930s. Note the following:

- Between the C7 and the F9 all of the notes move as little as possible, ensuring good voice leading: the E changes to E♭ and the B♭ changes to A, while the G and C remain the same.

- The B♭ played over the F7 chord in bar 6 is a dissonance. It is the same dissonance heard in bar 12 of Ex. 8, namely a perfect 4th above the root of the chord, which clashes with the 3rd of the chord.

- Though an anticipation occurs at the end of bar 6, one could have occurred earlier—at the end of bar 2 or bar 4, for example—but waiting until bar 6 for the first makes it more dramatic. It is subtle, but your listeners will notice. Anticipations require a minimum of technique, but they can make all the difference in the *feel* of your playing—and this is what will keep the audience wanting more.

- The major device used here to build excitement occurs in bars 9–10. These bars form the climax of the blues, the highest point of tension. Here you see a *condensation* of the pattern established and repeated four times in bars 1–8. Not only that, but bar 10 even condenses bar 9 by offering only one triplet figure (before the descending eighth notes [A–E]) instead of two. This creates a *rhythmic displacement*, in which a pattern occurs at a different place in the bar upon its second or subsequent appearance. In other words, the notes stay the same but the accentuation pattern changes.

- You can also add or subtract slides and anticipations, fine-tuning the amount of "push" you want. For example, you could anticipate the G7 by placing it on the "and" of beat 4 in bar 8. You might want to try taking out the slide that occurs before beat 3 in bars 1, 3, and 5, making your listeners wait until the beginning of the next bar for that little push. You have control over these subtle devices. Make a conscious use of them throughout your blues playing.

You can aim for ♩=120, but this example will still sound fine at a slower tempo.

CHAPTER 4

Creating Your Own Blues Riffs

You have seen how useful riffs are: as melodic units, they can carry a blues chorus along maintaining interest with little or no variation. From studying Exs. 5 and 6, you should be able to create your own rhythm-based riffs using right-hand chords. From Exs. 8 and 9 you have learned how to create melodic riffs using just the notes in the chords. Now you will learn an easy way to create your own melodic riffs with notes other than just chord tones.

Every note you play in the blues has a distinct meaning and carries a particular weight. The more you play, the more you will perceive the effects you can produce when you choose to use a 4th, a 6th, a ♭5th, etc. You will also understand how the same note on the keyboard assumes a different meaning when the underlying chord changes. It is a system in constant motion, which is what makes it so fascinating.

The way to grasp the meanings of notes is to learn a few at a time and incorporate them in your playing. When you acquire a sense of their unique sound, begin to add more notes to your palette.

You started with the four notes present in each of the I7, IV7, and V7 chords. Now you will add a five-note scale, the *pentatonic* scale. Whenever you feel overwhelmed with your note choices, or feel that you lack control over the meanings of your notes, you can always reduce the size of your note palette.

The Pentatonic Major Scale

The roots of the blues extend to West African music, which like many folk musics, is often based on pentatonic scales. These scales, free from half-steps, are extremely consonant. The easiest way to learn the pentatonic major scale is by its numerical formula. The formulas for scales are derived the same way as chord numbers: by counting up the major scale of the key, with the tonic of the key (the name of the key) as number one. While Roman numerals represent chords, Arabic numerals represent scale degrees. Both sets of numbers tell you the meaning, or function, of the note or chord within the context of the key in which you are playing. If you familiarize yourself with these numbers it will be easier to play the blues in different keys, which is essential in performance.

Below is a C major scale with the notes numbered. The numbers imply a series of intervallic relationships that are the same for every major scale, regardless of the key. Thus, the interval between 1 and 2 is always a major 2nd, between 1 and 4 is always a perfect 4th, etc. (Remember that every chord built on a note in that scale can also be named by Roman numeral.) This means that you need to learn the theory only once for all twelve keys. Then you need to practice them in *different keys* to get your hand and ear used to them.

Notice that there are only seven different notes. The top note, or tonic note, is simply an octave higher than the bottom note, so it has the same number.

Illustration 3

The C Pentatonic Major Scale

The pentatonic major scale formula is 1 2 3 5 6. Here is the C pentatonic major (C D E G A), fingered for the right hand. This is the simplest scale from which to create riffs.

Practicing The Pentatonic Major Scale

Practice the pentatonic major scale up and down the keyboard, from middle C to the very top and back down again, using the notated fingering. Play it in eighth notes with the metronome set at ♩=60, or even slower, if necessary. When you get back to your starting point, don't pause; just reverse direction and go up again. Do this 20 times before advancing the metronome. Then play the left-hand boogie pattern along with it, just staying on the C chord pattern.

Eighth-Note Swing Articulation

Why do professional blues players sound so good while amateurs, often playing the very same notes, sound so clunky? The answer often lies in *articulation*. The secret of a swinging, hip articulation—especially in a long line of eighth notes (as in Ex. 13)—is to accentuate the off-beats, namely the "ands" of traditional counting, as in 1-**&**-2-**&**-3-**&**-4-**&**. Use this articulation for all eighth-note melody lines. Practice this every day until it becomes natural to you. Most novices accent the downbeats (especially beat 1), which adds a corny weight to the line. Accenting the upbeats propels the line forward *without rushing* it. This is what you want.

Using Your Metronome On Beats 2 And 4

A metronome clicks away at a steady rate. What the clicks represent is up to the musician playing with it. Don't assume that each click has to be a quarter note. Blues and jazz musicians most often use the clicks of the metronome to designate the *backbeat* (beats 2 and 4) or, occasionally, the "ands" of each beat. This way, the perfectly even clicks of a metronome can be heard to swing. It takes some practice to hear the clicks this way, but don't give up. When you master this you will have strengthened your ability to swing.

Rearranging The Pentatonic Major Scale To Create A Riff

A *riff* is a short melodic idea that is repeated. Many blues songs are based on a single riff—a *riff blues*. The notes of the pentatonic major scale may be selected and rearranged to form many good blues riffs. The following illustration is a blues expression composed of notes from the pentatonic scale. This riff is then answered by another shorter expression that includes the ♭7 (borrowed from the C7 chord).

Illustration 4

This example begins with the call-and-response riff (shown above) and repeats it five more times. Notice that the riff is chromatically altered to fit the harmony in bars 5 and 9.

This riff blues illustrates a basic harmonic principle of the blues that you will learn to take much further: *The same notes played over the various chords creates a changing series of dissonances and resolutions.* Notice the different dissonances you get playing the riff over the V chord. The dissonance in the turnaround is particularly strong.

Improving A Riff Blues By Changing The Ending

A riff blues contains only a single phrase, and is thus the simplest melodic form of the blues (the chordal blues examples you played earlier were riff blues). Often, you can make your riff blues more powerful by changing the ending into a *response* to the riff. Just as one expression responded to another over two bars in Illustration 4, a different phrase (or a modification of the riff), beginning in bar 9, can create a larger-scale response to the rest of the chorus (bars 1–8).

Here, the riff blues from Ex. 11 is completed with a melodic resolution at the end. The resolution begins with the second half of the riff (shown with a bracket), a very economical gesture. Notice how satisfying it is. The repetition of the riff has set up a desire for change in the mind of the listener, an *expectation that something else will happen.* When you satisfy this expectation you generate pleasure. The fact that the change begins with an already familiar element makes it a particularly elegant solution, one that *grows* out of the preceding material. When you combine the new with the familiar you create particularly effective musical gestures.

Also, since the climax of this blues occurs in bars 9–10, the turnaround is less dramatic than the one in the previous example.

More Riffs

Here are some simple riffs based on the pentatonic major scale, with the occasional ♭7 (B♭) added. Remember to flat the E's when you play them over an F7 chord. (Note that in Ex. 13j the 3rd is flatted, even against the C chord. This creates a dissonance that is typical of the blues, one that you will learn more about in the next chapter.)

After you practice choruses based on the riffs in Ex. 13, you should make up your own pentatonic major–based riffs and write them down on a sheet of manuscript paper. Start out by trying variations on the riffs in Ex. 13, then try to come up with entirely new ones. The pentatonic scale lends itself to many melodic shapes.

A New Bass Pattern
To keep your blues from becoming stale and repetitive, you will need a number of resources. Particularly important is a variety of good-sounding bass patterns. Here is a new bass pattern to put under your belt.

Combining Riffs In A Different Way
This example features a combination of several of the riffs from Ex. 13. The first half of the riff (the call) keeps getting longer, while the second half (the response) stays the same. This is another way to combine the new with the familiar in such a way that the music *grows*.

INTERLUDE
The Deep Structure Of The Blues

Call and response is one of the oldest forms of music, ritual, theater, and dance. It harkens back, perhaps, to the early mirroring interactions between mother and child. A major secret of aesthetics is the mobilization of this ever-moving dialogue and the delicate balance it sets up between premonitions confirmed and premonitions overturned.

—Stephen Nachmanovitch, *Free Play*

Thematic Structure: The Blues' Power To Touch

Now that you have had some experience playing the blues, had a chance to develop a feel for its deeper structure and the way it tells a story, you understand that the blues is obviously more than just a 12-bar framework in which three chords appear in a particular pattern. Part of the blues' underlying structure is its *call-and-response* form (like the Biblical psalms), which occurs in a very particular three-part fashion. The parts of the overall call-and-response form are the three four-bar units introduced in Chapter 1. The first part (bars 1–4) constitutes the call, the second part (bars 5–8) is a repetition of the call, and the third (bars 9–12), is the response, or conclusion, including a climax. The call poses a question, or sets up an expectation; the repetition intensifies it with a new harmony; and the response answers, or fulfills it. Blues players have exercised their ingenuity to devise clever, interesting, compelling, beautiful, and energetic ways to confirm, delay, or frustrate those expectations.

The lyric of almost any blues articulates this structure. Here is what the first verse of a blues might be. Each line corresponds to a four-bar unit.

I woke up this mornin' feelin' sad and blue
I woke up this mornin' feelin' sad and blue
My gal's done left me, don't know what I'm gonna do

The third four-bar unit is the highly charged one and has the most going on in it. The listener has heard the same thing twice and is ready for something different, and the blues form really delivers.

Each four-bar unit has its own internal call-and-response pattern—on two levels: the first two-bars constitute the call and the second two, the response. This is clear in the above lyric where the words "I woke up this mornin'" occupy the first two bars, and "feelin' sad and blue" the second two. Many blues lyrics occupy only the first two bars, leaving the accompaniment to fill the second two bars. You can also do this instrumentally by playing a phrase during the first two bars and leaving the left hand to play by itself in the second two bars of each four-bar section.

With each two-bar unit you can also break the phrase down into its opening and closing cells, which occupy one bar apiece. Thus the call-and-response pattern works at three different levels of blues structure.

Harmonic Structure: The Blues' Power To Heal

The harmonic structure of the blues confirms and intensifies the pattern of tension and release in the melodic structure. Most non-blues music follows the overall pattern of consonance–dissonance–consonance. It begins by establishing a harmonic point of reference free of tension and generally based on the I chord. It then goes on to create tension with the use of other chords, which it resolves by eventually returning to the I chord.

In contrast to this, the harmonic structure of the blues *begins* in tension (pain) with the major/minor quality of the I chord. When the I chord *resolves* to the IV chord in bar 5 one feels a *decrease* in tension (relief from pain). The root movement (from I to IV) and the chord qualities (major/minor to 7th) reinforce this resolution of tension. Then going from I to V in bars 8–9, one experiences an *increase* in tension, which is then gradually resolved over bars 9–11. (Note also that musicians frequently play the IV chord in the *second* bar, returning to the I chord in bar 3, thus presenting a short, early excursion away from the home chord, which anticipates the longer excursion in the second four-bar unit.)

So, the transition from bar 4 to bar 5 in the blues structure constitutes a movement from the painful I chord to the healing IV chord. Is it any wonder that the blues became the essential medium for the expression of the African-American experience? This I-IV harmonic resolution is so typical of the blues that its use in any other musical context automatically suggests a bluesy feeling. Later you will see how the blues scale also supports this pattern of tension and release.

Telling A Story With The Blues

In order to make your blues playing "tell a story," you must bring your listeners into the music gradually. Start simply. Don't be afraid of playing *very few notes* (or chords) in the melody at the beginning; don't reveal everything you know at once. You might play a chorus of just the bass pattern, then a bar or even two with just a single note or chord in it. The next two bars might have two notes, and so on (more on this in Chapter 5). This focuses both you and your listener's attention on the music and prepares you both to go deeper. The jazz great Count Basie was a master of this understated approach.

You will also stay more *in control* of what you play if you start simply. Avoid the temptation to impress your listeners by playing your fastest, flashiest passage at the beginning. By starting simply you may surprise yourself at the originality of what you will eventually play. This is because you will be letting the deeper parts of your musical consciousness come out. You will also be giving yourself the time to find your bearings on the instrument before pumping out high-energy licks and phrases. Your listeners will really appreciate this approach. You may even receive praise you don't think you deserve at your technical level, yet you will have *moved* your listeners. This is what is most important.

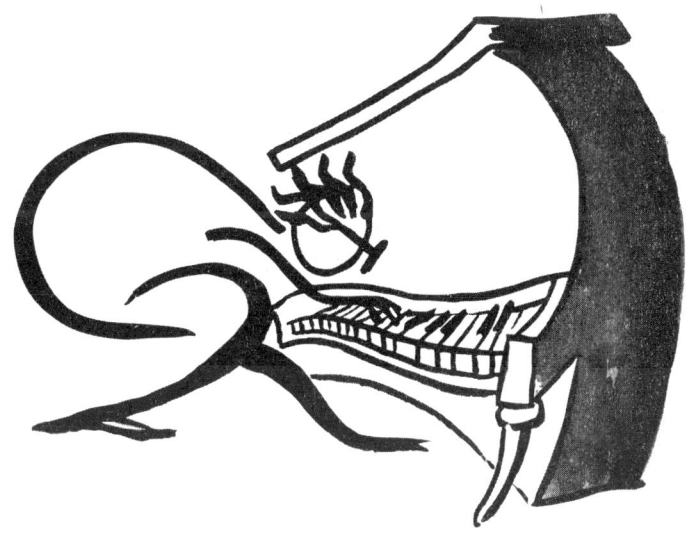

Chapter 5

The Blues Melodic Line I: A Subtractive Approach

The unconscious has infinite repertoires of structure already; all it needs is a little external structure on which to crystallize.
—Stephen Nachmanovitch, *Free Play*

Now you will learn how to create melodies using the blues scale. The blues scale is a marvelous device that sounds good over every chord in the blues progression. The fact that a single scale can work throughout a piece makes it easier to improvise in the blues than in other forms of music, such as jazz and popular.

Constructing The Blues Scale

Go back to the C pentatonic major scale in Ex. 10. Using this scale as your point of departure, perform the following steps:

1. Move the top note down an octave. This gives you a *pentatonic minor* scale—the A pentatonic minor to be exact. You may remember that A minor is the relative minor of C major. It has the same key signature (no sharps or flats). You simply start the pentatonic scale in a different place and it sounds minor.

2. Add the black key between the D and the E. This is adding the ♭5 between the 4 and the 5. Remember that A is now 1, since you're in A minor. This is the A blues scale.

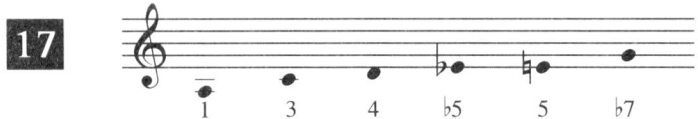

But we've been playing the blues in C! How do we find the C blues scale?

You've seen that the blues scale is constructed from the minor pentatonic with an added note. You just have to find the C minor pentatonic, which has the same notes as the major pentatonic of the *relative major* of C minor. C minor has three flats; E♭ major has three flats, so you need to examine E♭ pentatonic major.

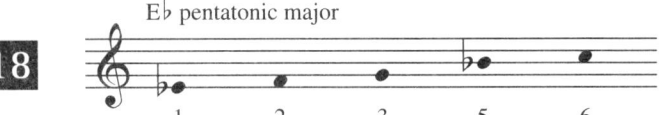
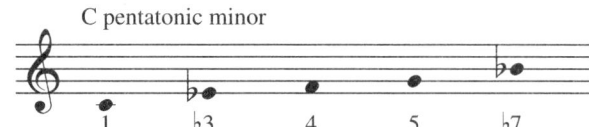

Now add the ♭5 (in the key of C), which is G♭ and there it is—the C blues scale!

Practicing The Blues Scale

This is the C blues scale, with a fingering.

You need to know the blues scale so well that you can almost play it in your sleep. Here's a way of learning it for automatic facility:

1. While using *eight-note swing articulation* (see Chapter 4) play the C blues scale up and down a single octave *in time*, as in Ex. 20. Notice the suggested fingerings. These may be varied to suit you (e.g., 3rd finger on the G♭).

2. Play the scale with the metronome, as slowly as you need to play it perfectly. Play the scale this way 20 times, *then* advance your metronome one notch each time you play the exercise until you begin making mistakes again, then stop. Resume later, a little slower than you finished the previous time. Start by playing only ten times, then advance your metronome one click, until you reach your tempo goal.

3. Play the scale up and down two octaves with your right hand. To do this, simply play the second C with your first finger rather than your fourth and repeat the fingering going up. Start at whatever tempo you can play it perfectly (even if it's a *painfully* slow tempo), and work up to ♩=120 (or even better, 𝅗𝅥=60, if you have your metronome clicking on beats 2 and 4).

4. Add the left-hand boogie pattern you've been using. Remember: Start at a much slower tempo when first playing hands together.

5. Play the blues scale all the way up and down the keyboard, reversing direction without stopping at the top of the keyboard, while playing the blues-form boogie bass. Aim for a tempo of ♩=132 for this one. Track 21 illustrates what this will sound like.

6. Now play the blues scale up and down the keyboard, except instead of using eighth notes as in Ex. 20, use *eighth-note triplets*. Track 22 illustrates what this will sound like.

7. Slow down if you need to. If you can play simple eighth notes well at ♩=132, triplets should be no problem at a somewhat slower speed. Then work back up to ♩=132. If you can't play the triplets, go back to the eighth notes, slow them down to a *comfortable* tempo and gradually increase their speed. *If you are not relaxed at the speed you're playing an exercise, then you're playing it too fast.*

Understanding The Blues: Harmonic Tension And Release In The Blues Scale

Let's look at each note in the blue scale against the I, IV, and V chords, and tally up the dissonances (which create tension) and consonances (which establish resolution). Deciding when to use consonance or dissonance is essential to creating drama in a blues improvisation.

Over the C7, or I7, chord:
- The 1 (C) is consonant.
- The ♭3 (E♭) is dissonant.
- The 4 (F) is dissonant.
- The ♭5 (G♭) is dissonant.
- The 5 (G) is consonant.
- The ♭7 (B♭) is consonant.

That makes three dissonances and three consonances over the C7 chord.

Now the same for the F7, or IV7, chord:
- The 1 (C) is consonant (the 5 of the chord).
- The ♭3 (E♭) is consonant (the ♭7 of the chord).
- The 4 (F) is consonant (the 1 of the chord).
- The ♭5 (G♭) is dissonant (the ♭2 or ♭9 of the chord).
- The 5 (G) is consonant (the 9th of the chord).
- The ♭7 (B♭) is dissonant (the 4 of the chord).

Here the score is two to four, dissonances to consonances. Fewer dissonances and more consonances strengthen the feeling of resolution following the first chord. This is one of the keys to the sound of the blues: *the blues begins and ends with the tension of the tonic chord.* The tension resolves briefly with the IV chord.

Here is the G7, or V7, chord tally:
- The 1 (C) is dissonant (the 4 of the chord).
- The ♭3 (E♭) is dissonant, (the ♭13 of the chord).
- The 4 (F) is consonant (the ♭7 of the chord).
- The ♭5 (G♭) is *very* dissonant (♮7 of the chord).
- The 5 (G) is consonant (the 1 of the chord).
- The ♭7 (B♭) is dissonant (the ♭3 of the chord [often called the ♯9]).

This chord is the most dissonant of all, with four dissonances and two consonances.

Why It's Easy To Improvise The Blues

You don't have to think about these consonant/dissonant relationships; they happen *automatically* when you're playing melodic lines. This is an amazing feature of the blues: the melodic material can be very simple, even repetitive, but played against the background of the changing blues chords, it takes on rich meaning. This is why it's easy to begin improvising in the blues.

Improvising With The Blues Scale

Now that you can play the blues scale continuously, up and down the keyboard, at a steady tempo, you can begin to create forms and to shape lines out of it—all while playing the boogie bass in the left hand, of course.

Each step in this process adds an element of freedom. The step-by-step method allows you to experiment with each new element to consider what sounds good. Always aim for a mixture of repetition and change, predictability and surprise. Notated musical examples are omitted here because the idea is to relate *directly to the keyboard*, guided only by your ear. Become aware of the new elements you have at your command as you work with each stage. Here are the steps:

1. *Mix Rhythms*—First mix up eighth notes and triplets in your lines. Try not to repeat a pattern more than two or three times. Listen to Track 23. **23**

2. *Reverse Direction*—Reverse direction anywhere during your movement up or down the keyboard. This includes quick reversals after two, three, four, etc., notes and back again. Listen to Track 24. **24**

3. *Add Leaps*—Experiment with leaps by playing notes in succession that are not next to each other in the Listen to the sound of every interval in the blues scale. Each interval has a particular meaning. Note especially the effect of the tritone ♭5–1 going up and the use of octaves. Notice how effective repeating the same note can be too. Listen to Track 25. **25**

4. *Add Space*—Finally, put in spaces—rests. This will break up your continuous stream of notes into discrete phrases. The rests may be short or long; experiment with both; mix up different lengths. Listen to Track 26. **26**

As you continue playing, you will develop a feeling for making statements, repeating them, and varying them.

Finding The Blues Scale In Any Key

Of course, you will need to be able to play the blues in several (if not all) keys. To find the blues scale of any key, follow this procedure:

1. Find the major scale that begins a minor 3rd above your target tonic. This will be the relative major.
2. Play the 1st, 2nd, 3rd, 5th, and 6th degrees of this major scale.
3. Bring the 6th degree down an octave. This is your target tonic. You now have a pentatonic minor in your target key.
4. Add the ♭5.

By looking at the C blues scale (Ex. 19), you might decide that it's easier just to find the notes by applying the 1 ♭3 4 ♭5 5 ♭7 directly to the major scale. Either way, the result is the same.

The Blues Scale In Other Keys

You already know the A blues scale; here are six more blues scales, with fingerings. Notice how easy the blues scales are in the "sharp" keys. (Play the top note with your first finger if you are continuing up, or with the notated finger if you are coming back down.)

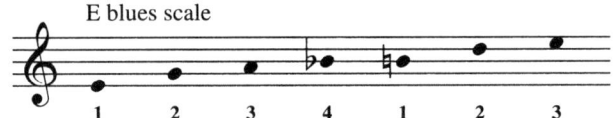

Finding The I, IV, And V Chords In Other Keys

To find the I, IV, and V chords in any key, simply play the major scale of that key and construct dominant 7th-type chords on the 1st, 4th, and 5th degrees of the scale. You are using those notes as *roots* to form new chords. Remember that dominant 7th-type chords have a major 3rd on the bottom, with two minor 3rds stacked on top.

Another way of looking at it is to play the major triad on the bottom and find the 7th by counting down two half-steps from the octave above the root of the chord. In the key of F, for example, the chords for the blues are F7 (F A C E♭), B♭7 (B♭ D F A♭), and C7 (C E G B♭).

Try to tackle a new key every week or so, depending on your practice schedule. Go through the same procedure to learn each new blues scale. This way you'll be playing in several keys in a fairly short time.

Creating Musical Meaning

Dynamics

Don't neglect the other ways to create musical meaning. You already know about *articulation* and the method of accenting the notes on the off-beats. The *overall* dynamics—the relation between soft and loud sections—is an extremely powerful tool as well. You can play the same chorus twice, making the loud parts soft and the soft parts loud, the second time, and fascinate your listeners without changing a note! Again, this is making the familiar new by expressing the same musical material in a different way.

Repetition/Variation

When you are improvising you're playing melodies you've never played before. Consequently, your listeners have never heard them before, so they need some *repetition* to hold onto, to create some familiarity, to perceive that what you're playing is indeed a logical statement.

As you master the blues scale, you develop a powerful tool for generating melodies. The trick is to make those notes significant, and the most effective means to do that is through repetition.

Start by repeating short, simple ideas—two to three notes at most. The ease with which your listener grasps them acts in your favor. Keep a notebook of your best blues phrases and learn them in all keys. This will increase your capacity to build larger phrases from smaller ones. Repeat your phrase or riff two or three times, then vary it.

Many beginning players may find they have the opposite problem—falling into a pattern and unable to get out. Typically, this kind of pattern involves starting phrases at the same place in a one-bar or two-bar unit, time after time. Some people don't even notice that they're doing it. The remedy is to become aware of the particular beats of the bar on which you are beginning and ending, and to change them. (You will learn a systematic solution to this problem in the next chapter.)

Change Of Register

By jumping an octave (or more) between phrases you can add a burst of energy to your solo. In the same way, if you extend a phrase downward into the register just below middle C and stay there for a complete chorus, you can add depth and power to your blues.

Assignment

Before you begin the next section, learn the blues scale and the boogie bass in at least one other key—F. Then, take on subsequent keys at a pace that is comfortable: one per week if you practice an hour or more per day. Take longer if you don't practice as much.

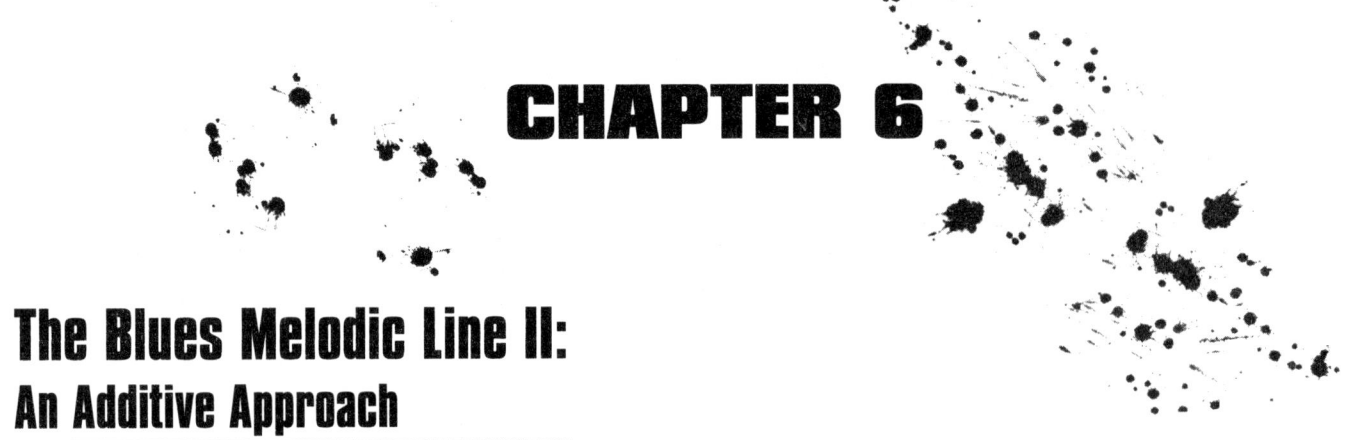

CHAPTER 6

The Blues Melodic Line II: An Additive Approach

Now that you have acquired skill playing the blues scale in at least one key, you will always have *something* to play to fill your blues solos. The true art of the blues, however, is in playing lines, phrases, and solos that *touch* the audience—playing that communicates deep feeling, exposes your soul, and penetrates the souls of your listeners.

The temptation, once you can play the blues scale fluently, is to play continuous lines too frequently. The art is in knowing what *not* to play—*less is more*. The *additive* approach will help you develop this skill.

This approach begins with a single note and shows you how to build up phrases based on what you hear inside you and ultimately what you feel. You already know the blues scale, so you have something to play to express a feeling. Now you will learn how to wait for that feeling or idea before playing it. When you can do this consistently, you will reach a new level of communication through the blues.

The Eighth Note "Beats"

This is an exercise that will expand your rhythmic vocabulary by using a very simple device that can be practiced even away from the piano.

Imagine a bar of 4/4 divided into eight eighth notes: 1-&-2-&-3-&-4-&. Now imagine two of these bars strung together, with the notes numbered one through eight in each bar. These are the *eighth note "beats,"* and you have two sets of them in this two-bar unit. Each eighth note "beat" has its own rhythmic identity and therefore has the potential to create a specific musical meaning.

Illustration 5

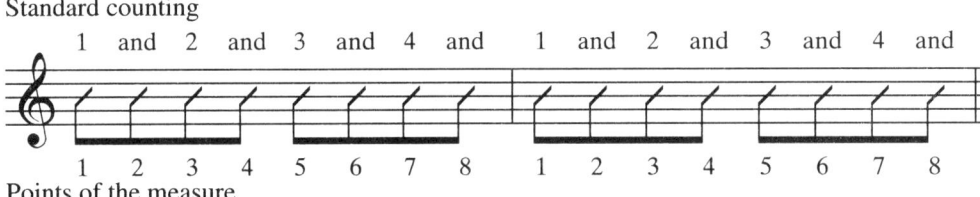

Creating Your Own Patterns

The next exercise will be to create eight rhythmic patterns over this two-bar unit, each one beginning on each of the eight "beats" of the first bar. Your rhythm will consist of an alternating mixture of hits (notes), which you'll tap with your hand, and rests.

1. While counting to eight repeatedly, clap a particular rhythm, starting at the first point and tapping through the two-bar unit in a mixture of taps and rests. Try to create a rhythm as syncopated and hip as possible, using relatively few claps and a lot of space (rests). Keep doing this until you arrive at a rhythm you like.

2. Repeat the rhythm you have created until you have memorized it, then write it down, with or without music paper. (You can just write the numbers 1 through 8 twice on a line, then circle the numbers where you put the hits or claps.)

3. Do this eight times, one for each "beat" in the first bar. You will be surprised at how many interesting rhythms you'll come up with when you work this way.

Here are two examples on the first two "beats" to give you an idea.

Review these patterns over several days so that they become part of your rhythmic vocabulary. This will enrich your blues playing (and every other type of playing you do) tremendously.

An additive process begins with space (empty bars) and inserts note-events. Notice the amount of space left in the bars. This approach reveals each note's power—derived as much from the note's rhythmic placement as from its pitch—to bear an emotional message. In the subtractive approach you learned how never to run out of notes, but it always runs the risk of encouraging automatic playing. The additive approach shows you how you can invest each note with meaning, to *feel*, and to *intend* every note.

The One-Note Blues

Now that you have a repertoire of at least eight two-bar rhythmic patterns, go to your keyboard and set the metronome to a comfortable tempo, and play the first pattern on a single note in the right hand. Next play this adding the left-hand boogie pattern, and you have the one-note blues.

Play your pattern first in every pair of bars (1–2, 3–4, 5–6, etc.), then at the beginning of each four-bar section, fill the second two-bar half of the section with your own improvised answer—still playing on a single note. The first half of each section is your prepared material, and the second half is your spontaneous material. This will give you both a stable form and a stimulus for generating new ideas.

After you have explored the possibilities of this first pattern, try your second one the same way. Make a table in your practice log book to keep track of your progress through this exercise, with a column for the pattern number (1–8), a column to check off when you have performed that pattern during a blues chorus every two bars, and a column to check off when you have performed it every other two bars, inserting new improvised material in between.

Pattern Number	Every Two Bars	Every Other Two Bars
1	_____	_____
2	_____	_____
3	_____	_____
etc.		

After you have gone through at least four of the eight, eight-point patterns you have collected, try improvising on a single note throughout the whole 12-bar blues form. You may be surprised to find how coherent your playing is. *This is not just an exercise.* Repeated notes build intensity. They create a very effective dramatic device. Use them in performance!

You will know when you are ready to go on to the next step when you begin hearing blues melodic phrases inside your head.

Expanding The One-Note Blues

For the next step, play a two-note blues using just the tonic and an adjacent note from the blues scale (either C and B♭, or C and E♭). Use your patterns and see how much music you can make from just these two notes. Then go beyond your patterns, improvising new ones.

Tip: Don't alternate the two notes back-and-forth all the time. Repeat one of them for a while, then introduce the other one as a change after you have reached a saturation point. This is called *growth* in music, the process of widening the scope. It is a very satisfying effect, but you must prepare for it by exploring a limited field first, in this case a single pitch.

Here is a two-note example based on the second line from Ex. 28. Play it over the blues progression, as on the recording.

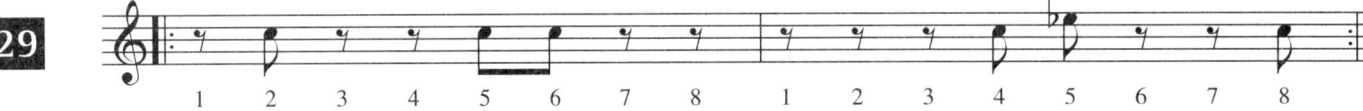

At this point you may decide to stay with your patterns or to improvise your rhythms freely, depending on how confident you feel. Either way, the next step is to add one more note. Explore the three-note blues using the techniques of repetition and suspense you learned with the two-note blues. Then add a fourth note, and so on. This is an excellent strategy to use in performance, chorus by chorus, to build excitement. Take at least a whole chorus to explore each stage. As an exercise, of course, you can stay on a particular level for much longer, as long as a week, which would greatly intensify the experience.

In performance, the more you repeat a note, or even a short phrase, the more tension you build, and the more power you invest in whatever you do to break that tension. Thus, the simplest phrase can make a profound impression if it comes after a long tense repetitive build-up—or a long silence.

Blues Scale Phrases

Here is a group of blues phrases, all in the key of C (Exs. 30–40). Learn them, then transpose them to the other keys in which you play the blues. Remember to play eighth notes with a swing feel and articulation.

Use these phrases as the building blocks for riff-based blues choruses by playing them as written in bars 1–2 and 5–6, then varying them somewhat in bars 9–10. In the intervening bars you can either pause or add a response of your own. Exs. 32 and 33 include pickups that are played before the first bar of the blues form, or, if played inside the form, in the even-numbered bars. Each example is played twice, once alone and once with left-hand accompaniment.

31

32

33

34

35

36

37

38

39

40

Another Left-Hand Alternative

This is a non–boogie-woogie, left-hand accompaniment pattern based on the Charleston rhythm (♪ ❜ ❜ ♪ ♩). When you master it, you will be on your way to developing the rhythms of jazz comping (accompanying). Practice your left hand alone, then take any example from 30–40 and make a riff blues out of it; see if you can keep the two rhythms going independently. (You may have to change registers of one hand or the other to prevent clashes.)

Notice that the IV chord appears in the second bar, interrupting the usual four bars of the I chord. This is a very common alternative chord progression. It offers a short departure from the home chord as a "preview" of what is to happen in bar 5. You are probably already familiar with it from listening to the blues.

Adding Contrast And Variation To Blues Phrases

It is as great an art to *develop* your own musical idea or phrase as it is to come up with a new one. By exploring ways to vary a phrase, you learn how to draw out the maximum emotional meaning from that phrase, and from your instrument. Here is a list of ways to add variety to your playing. Ex. 41, following this list, uses phrases from Exs. 30–40 to illustrate the following principles of contrast, variation, and transformation. Come up with similar examples on your own.

1. Keep in mind the following ways to add contrast to your playing.

    - *Low/High*. Finish a phrase then jump to another part of the keyboard for the next phrase.

    - *Dense/Sparse*. Alternate playing just a few notes in a bar with playing many notes.

    - *Soft/Loud*. The same phrase can gain new meaning when played at a different dynamic (loudness) level.

    - *Repeated/Varied*. As a call-and-response form, the blues sets up expectations that a phrase-statement will be answered. These expectations are intensified when the original phrase is repeated. The most typical pattern is for a phrase to occur twice before an answer is given. The only rule is that the more times a phrase is repeated, the higher the expectation of change—but also the greater the risk of boredom. The answer or response can be a completely new phrase that somehow complements the first phrase, or it can be a variation on the first phrase.

2. Try the following ways to vary your phrases.

- *Addition.* Repeat the phrase, but add more notes to it.

- *Condensation.* Repeat the phrase, but leave out notes from the inside—or speed them up so they fit into less space.

- *Truncation.* Repeat the phrase, but stop before you come to the end. Again, this works well the third time you play the phrase.

3. More advanced principles of transformation.

- *Expansion*: Play the same notes over a longer period of time.

- *Sequencing*: Repeat a phrase starting on a different note of the scale, while maintaining the similar intervallic relationships between the notes.

- *Expanding Intervals*: Keep the same high/low relationships between your notes, but widen the intervals between them.

- *Condensing Intervals*: Same as above, but narrow the intervals.

- *Rhythmic Displacement.* Start the repetition of a phrase at a different place in the bar. For example, if the original phrase began on the beat 2, begin its repetition on the beat 1 of the following bar. (See Chapter 7, "Shifting Accent Groupings.")

A Composite Example

This example gives you practice with the Charleston rhythm and using the IV chord in the second bar. In the right hand, the first chorus illustrates a typical unfolding of a blues phrase: it begins with two simple blues licks (Exs. 30 and 31), and ends with Ex. 32 and a variation on Ex. 40. The second chorus contains a number of the other principles (see if you can identify each of the techniques) for illustration purposes, but in a real performance, any one or two of them would be sufficient content for a chorus.

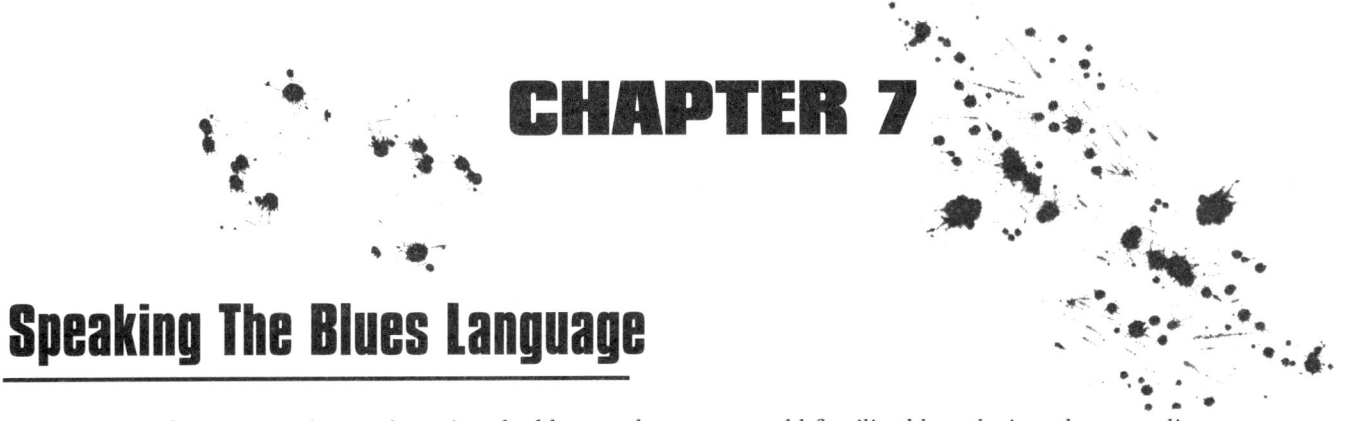

CHAPTER 7

Speaking The Blues Language

Now that you can improvise using the blues scale, you can add familiar blues devices that your listeners expect to hear. They reassure your listeners that they are in comfortable territory, and that they can trust you to make authentic statements in the idiom—plus they are fun and easy to play.

DRAMATIC DEVICES

Some of the most beloved and familiar sounds of the blues are also some of the easiest to play. If you can improvise using the blues scale, you have mastered the hard part. Now for some gravy.

Trills And Tremolos

Trills and tremolos are the pianist's emotional equivalents of *wails*, those long, mournful notes that are so expressive on horns, especially saxophones. Because the piano can't sustain notes like a horn, pianists have used trills and tremolos to produce long, intense sounds. Trills and tremolos sound best at the beginning or end of a melody.

A *trill* is a rapid alternation between two notes a half step or a whole step apart. The most common trill in the blues is between the ♭7 and the 1.

A *tremolo* or shake is the rapid alternation between any two or more notes more than a step apart. Ex. 43 illustrates this with a minor 3rd, but it will work well with the notes of any interval in the blues scale, as well as with the tritone between the ♭3 and the 6 (E♭ and A in the key of C) and some other intervals in the major scale. Use your ear to find out what works. Also, try every trill and tremolo in all registers above middle C, not just in the one written in the example. As always, transpose these to the other keys.

Remember that a single, repeated note is a type of tremolo, one that builds a special kind of intensity. Try repeating any single note rapidly, using the fingering 4-3-2-1, 3-2-1, or 3-1. This works especially well with the 5th of any scale (for example, G in the key of C).

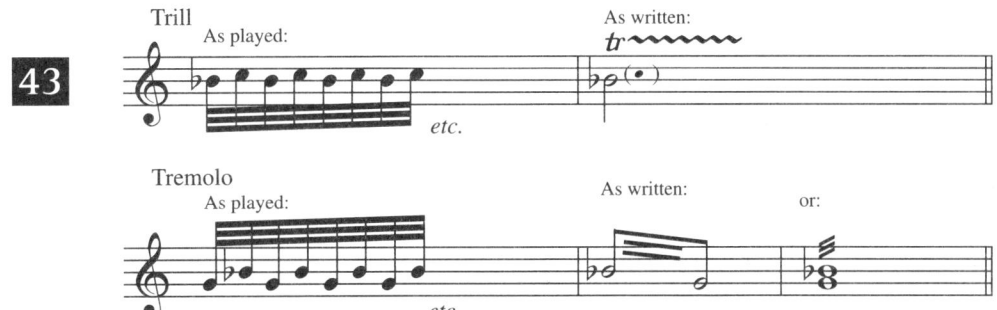

This is an example of how you might use a tremolo to begin or to end a phrase. Notice that the tremolo is used on all of the long, held notes.

You can also use tremolos or shakes on chords. It can be very powerful to shake all the notes of the chord in the right hand before moving into a line.

This example introduces you to the 7#9 chord—a powerfully dissonant chord, highly characteristic of the major/minor duality of the blues—and to the 9th chord, which simply adds the 9th (the same as the 2nd, but it functions as an extension of the dominant seventh).

Repeating Patterns And Cluster Tremolos

Certain repeating patterns are so characteristic of the blues they practically define the blues sound. They are very easy to execute, and they add authenticity to your sound. Many of them incorporate blue notes alongside adjacent notes, so they are quite similar to the blues slides. Here, however, instead of playing the blues slide as a grace note, articulate each note as a separate, but even, rhythmic value.

When you speed up any of these patterns they become *cluster tremolos*, which grab the ear with their continuous dissonance.

Though some of these licks are written as sextuplets and some as triplets, try them all at different speeds, but keep all notes distinct and well articulated, even at higher speeds. Play them only as fast as you can articulate them clearly.

Once you have learned these, make up some of your own.

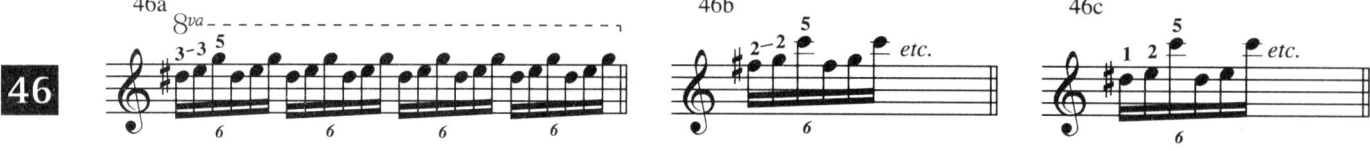

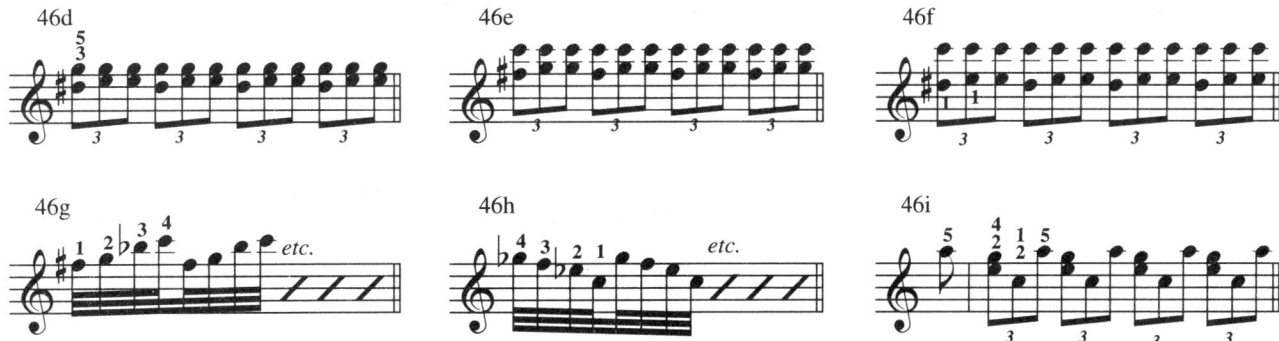

Shifting Accent Groupings

If you play a pattern in which the number of notes is different from the number of beats, the accents will fall in a different place each time the pattern is repeated. This is very simple once you catch on—and it is highly effective.

For example, you can play a four-note repeating pattern as a series of triplets (or a three-note repeating pattern in groups of four sixteenth notes). The first, or accented, note of each four-note group will then fall at a different place in the triplet, producing a *rhythmic displacement*. You can either accent the first note of each triplet, or the first note of each four-note group. Each approach will produce a slightly different displacement effect. You can play this device in groups of four triplets, completing an entire pattern cycle when the first note of the four-note group falls on the first beat of the triplet, as illustrated in Exs. 47–52.

(Note: In Ex. 51 the four-note pattern is not repeated exactly, but the effect of accent displacement is still present. Exs. 53 and 54 illustrate three-note patterns played in groups of four sixteenth notes.)

ENDINGS

Endings Should Be Dramatic

Endings are one of the most familiar and best-loved elements of a good blues performance. You can use some kind of ending material at the end of each blues chorus, but if you do this every time your choruses will sound too predictable. The very end of a blues performance piece should be as dramatic as possible. In fact, the chord on which you end may be the most complex chord of your whole performance—you don't want to leave your audience with too much consonance! Ending devices may be a bit more complicated than the rest of the music you have learned so far. They are worth the effort: they are the last thing your listeners hear.

Exs. 55–59 offer some suggested endings. Each should start in bar 11 of the blues. Ex. 55 is the most traditional, and uses a grace-note slide up to a single bass note in the left hand. Note that if you take the first ending in that example, you can go back to the top of the blues form for the subsequent chorus(es). Then use the last ending to end that particular piece. Exs. 56 and 57 are other traditional endings. Exs. 58 and 59 are endings that use the blues scale. Try to create more endings like these. (Note: Exs. 55–58 begin in the penultimate bar of the blues form, bar 11. Ex. 59 begins in bar 9.)

Putting Repeating Patterns In Context

This blues chorus illustrates the use of repeating patterns. Notice that they don't always fit conveniently into a single bar: In bars 5 and 7 the patterns start after the downbeat; in bars 6, 8, and 10 the pattern "bleeds" over from the previous bar; and in the latter two cases it expands as well. All this gives the music a feeling of continuous flow.

CHAPTER 8

Adding Variety

Varieties Of Blues Experience

There are many blues forms and chord progressions. Besides the 12-bar form, the blues is played in an 8-bar form, a 16-bar form, and a form that includes a bridge. The bebop musicians of the 1940s worked out elaborate chord substitutions for the blues. You can see one set of them in Ex. 77. The blues is found in many different types of rhythm settings, including rock, funk, and even Latin music. At the beginning or intermediate level you can stay with a single chord structure within the 12-bar form, but there are two areas where you can add variety to fill out your performance: openings and bass patterns.

More Bass Patterns

Below are some more bass patterns for solo piano. Most of them come right out of the boogie-woogie tradition and are associated with a particular artist's style or a particular piece. (Remember that when you play in a band, you need to simplify your left hand or leave the patterns to the bass player.) The basic patterns are shown here, presenting only one or, at most, two bars of the pattern, but on the recording they are used in the context of complete blues choruses.

Each example is played in three ways on the recording:

- By itself, at a slow tempo for four bars.
- With a right-hand melody line.
- With a right-hand melody for an *entire* blues chorus, and at a quicker tempo.

Swing Eighths vs. Even Eighths

Until now you have been playing with swing eighths exclusively, but you can also play the blues with *straight eighth notes* to get a different and exciting sound. Bass lines are a good place to start experimenting with a "straight" feel. Listen to the recording for examples of both approaches.

Playing A Bass Pattern By Itself

Playing a left-hand bass pattern alone for the first four bars, or even for the entire first chorus, is an effective way to introduce a blues. It is dramatic to have the right-hand enter in bar 5, emphasizing the change to the IV chord, especially if you use an anticipation in bar 4. The more complex bass patterns, such as Exs. 62, 63, 66, 67, 68, 70, and 71, work best with this approach. Exs. 72–76 are New Orleans–style R&B bass patterns, which are based on Latin-type syncopations.

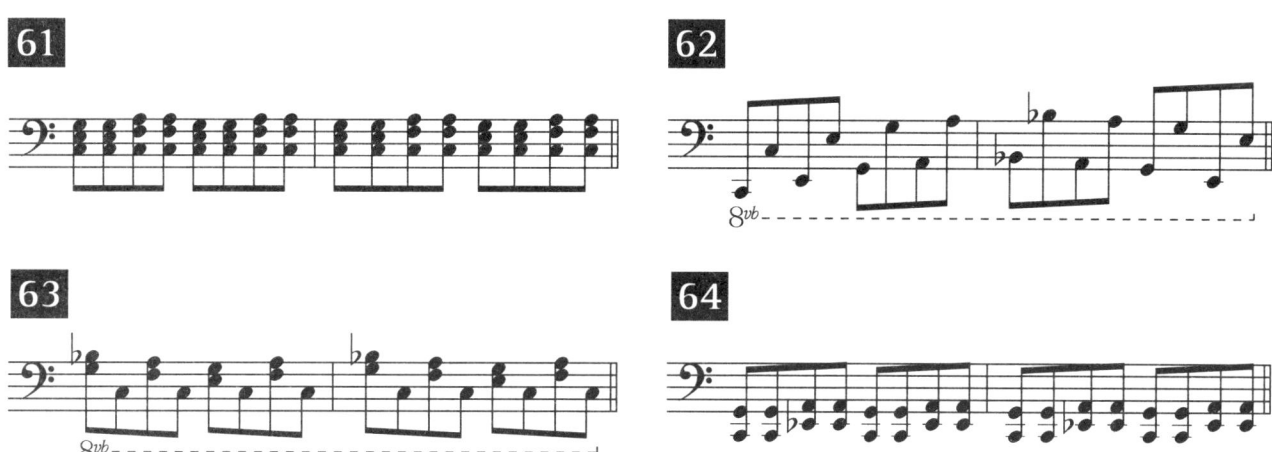

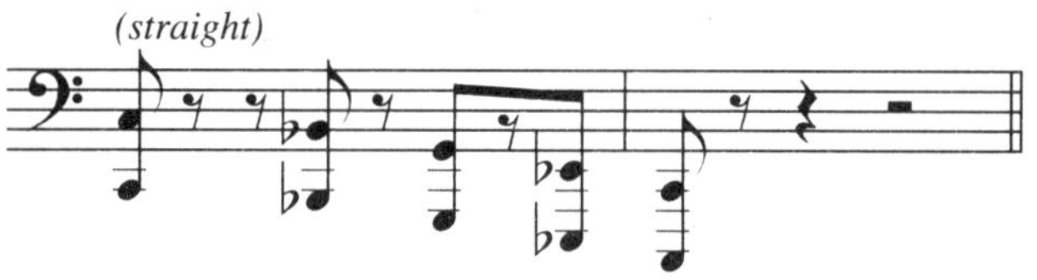

The Blues Ballad

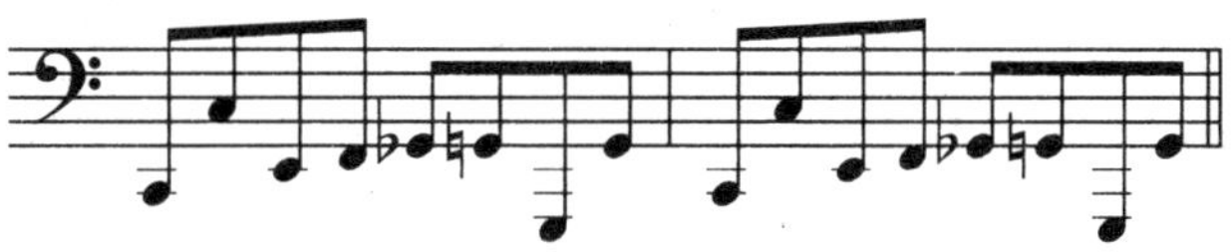

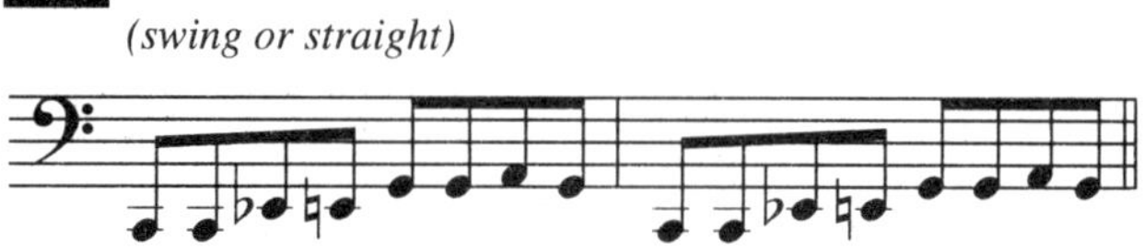

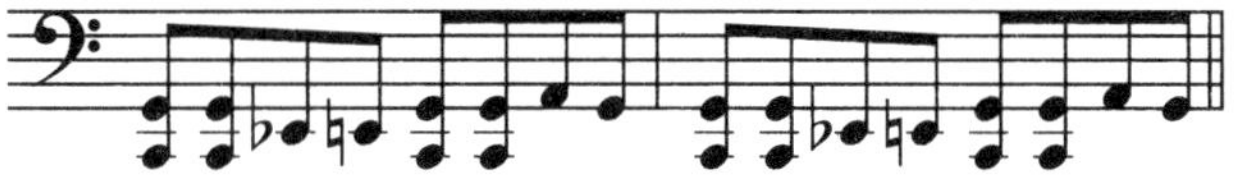

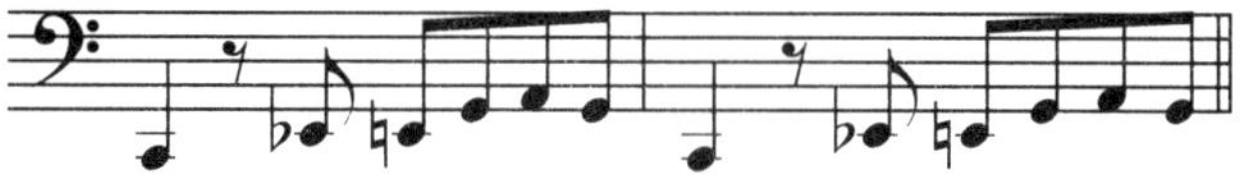

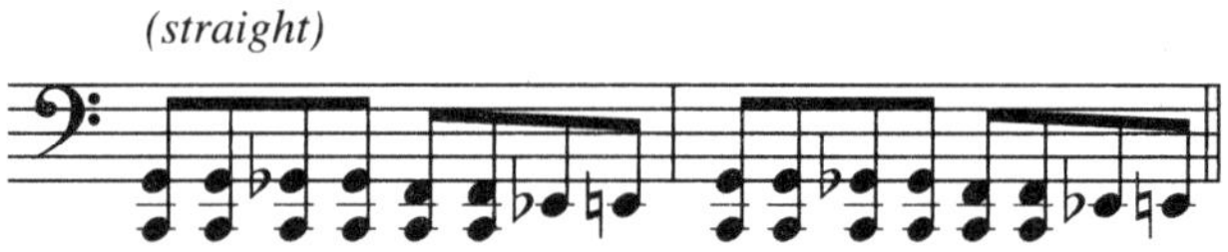

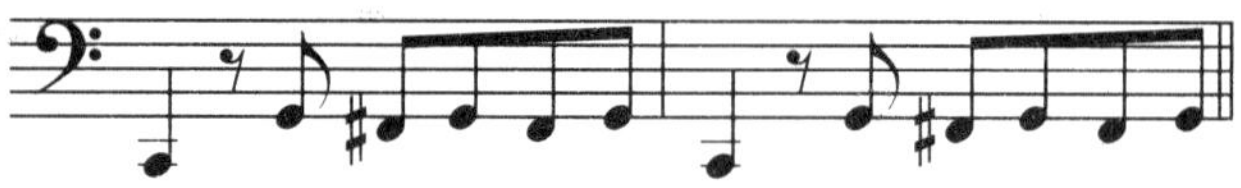

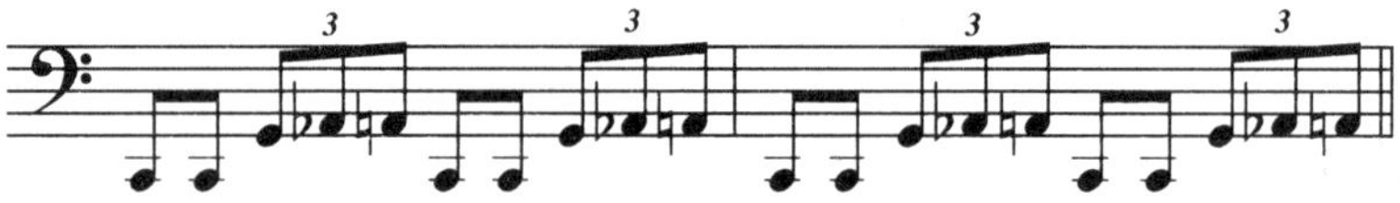

A slow blues can also be played like a ballad by using a different kind of bass entirely. Ex. 77 illustrates a basic swing bass, which consists primarily of single notes on beats 1 and 3, and chords in the middle register on beats 2 and 4. In some transitional bars, bass notes are used on the beat 4 to lead into the chord of the following bar. At a more advanced level you can use octaves or 10ths instead of the single notes. This example illustrates the use of alternate chord changes in bars 8–10. These changes are especially popular in jazz versions of the blues. They are presented here in the slow context of a ballad so you can learn them more easily, but they work in fast (non-boogie) blues too.

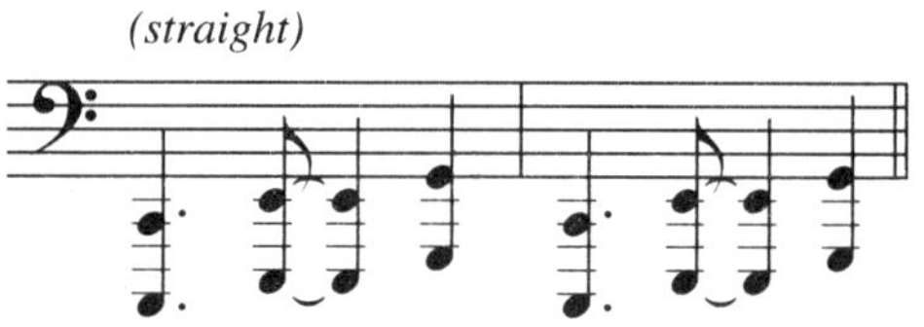

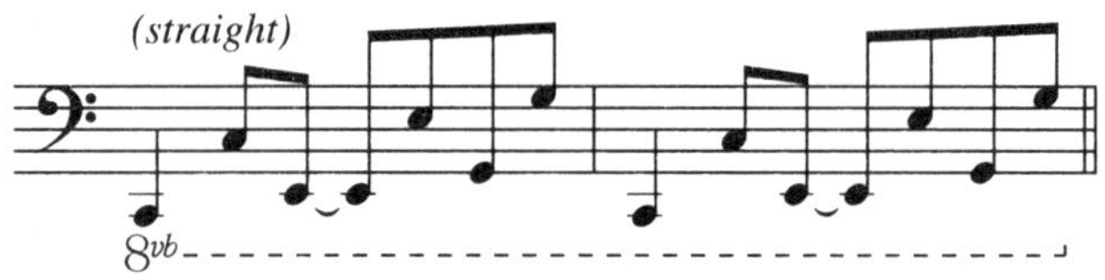

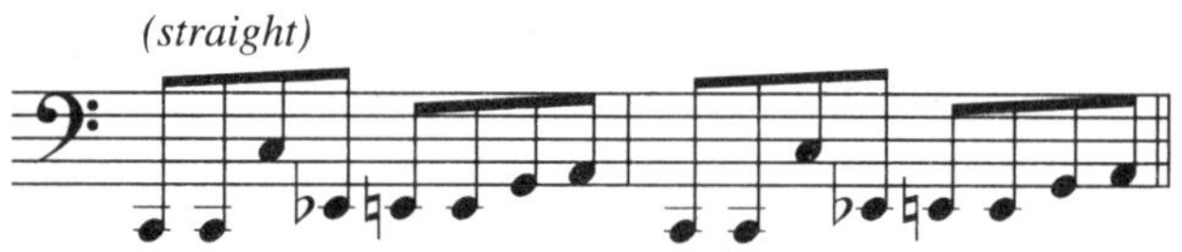

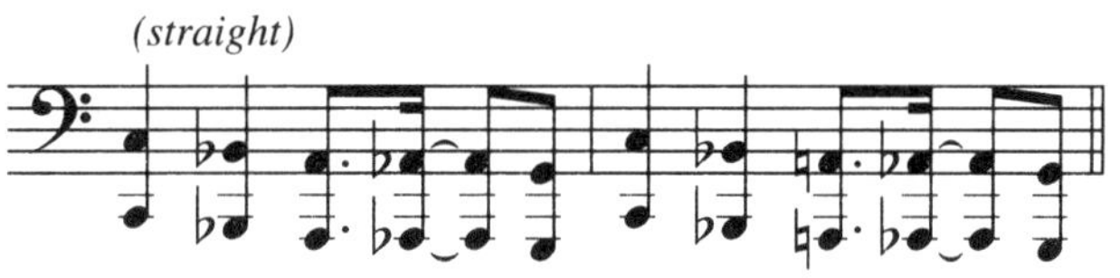

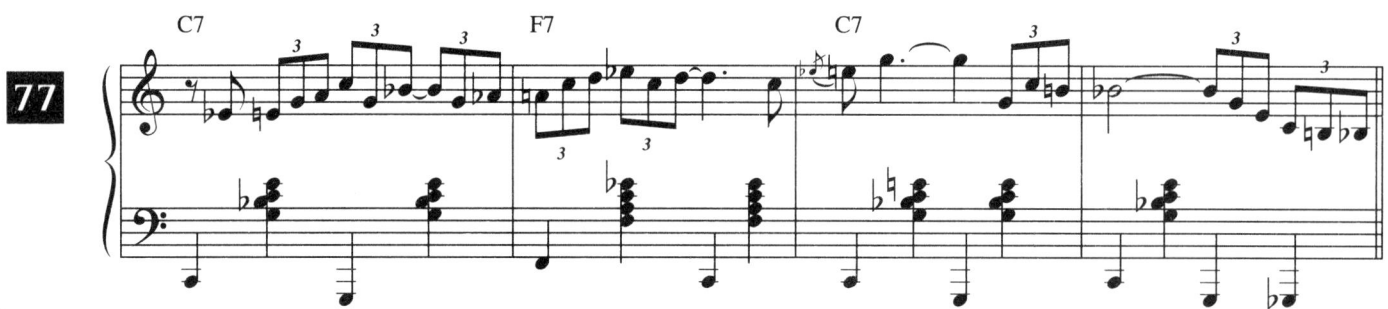

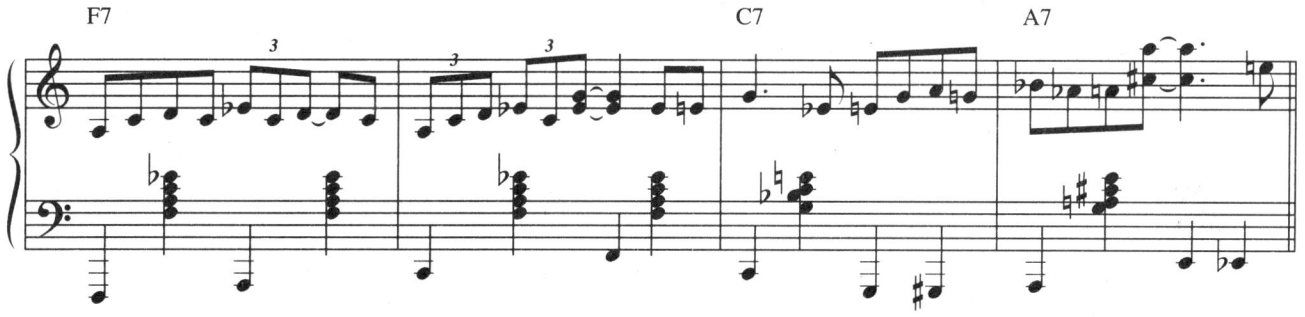

Accompanying A Vocalist

Once you have mastered several bass patterns in several keys you will be ready to accompany a blues singer–perhaps yourself! Just play an appropriate left-hand pattern with chords in the right hand. Begin with the Charleston rhythmic pattern discussed in Chapter 2. Then see if you can play chords in the spaces left by the singer, keeping in mind the principle of call-and-response. Next, add fills made up of blues phrases and dramatic devices.

If you can play solo blues piano, accompanying singing is easy. The most important thing is to stay out of the singer's way and not double the singer's melody.

Alternative Openings

This dramatic, attention-getting opening is an alternative to the simple opening described in "Playing A Bass Pattern By Itself" (p.45). Here, over the opening four bars of your first chorus, a single-line melody in both hands is played two octaves apart.

This riff is a variation on Ex. 78, using a *backbeat* in the left hand, against octaves in the right.

This example extends the form with this very popular opening. Here, the four-bar section on the tonic chord has been expanded to eight bars, making a 16-bar blues. The rest of the form remains the same.

CODA

The requisite variety that opens up our expressive possibilities comes from practice, play, exercise, exploration, experiment. The effects of non-practice (or of insufficiently risky practice) are rigidity of heart and body and an ever-shrinking compass of available variety.

—Stephen Nachmanovitch, *Free Play*

Where To Go From Here

If you have studied the material in this book and learned it well, you have enough skill to play very respectable blues piano. You can now improvise the blues, and you can understand more of what you hear. But this is only the beginning, eventually you will be able to play a blues idea after hearing it only once or twice.

Continue to keep a notebook of favorite phrases and ideas that you pick up from other players or that you compose. It is beneficial to know a small number of these phrases very well so that you can play them instantly, whenever you need them. You can always build on them during a performance.

You also have the tools to investigate other blues and related styles. Listen for such blues types as the shuffle blues, the blues ballad, the blues waltz, the minor blues, the New Orleans–style blues, the many types of gospel music, soul, rock, and jazz. There are many excellent method books on other styles (see the *Suggested Reading*), and of course the music itself is everywhere. Above all, *listen*. Attend live performances and move with the music.

There are many excellent books for intermediate players as well (see *Suggested Reading*). You should learn complete blues performances directly from recordings, either writing the music down or not. This is what all serious players do. Work from a two-speed tape deck, or a digital music source, such as a sequencer or MIDI file. With some MIDI sequences, you can learn directly from experts (look under "Computer Programs" in the *Suggested Reading*). Imitate every lick, and every nuance of your source; capture the entire sound (articulation, rhythmic subtleties, and dynamics), not just the pitches.

Take sections of what you learn and transpose them to all keys. Insert this material in your playing; play off it. Develop a repertoire of blues licks, a pool that you can draw from instantaneously—whenever you play, in whatever key. Remember: It is better to know a few things very well than to know many things approximately.

Performance Attitude

Many amateur musicians suffer from performance anxiety. It is a widespread condition, but it need not hold you back. If you have practiced sufficiently and you are still nervous playing in front of people, here are a few things to keep in mind:

1. You're It!

In most instances you are the only live player around. It is you or nothing . . . or recorded music, which is just for background in most cases. The audience is grateful to you for playing, they are on your side, willing to hear what you have to say. If you are not Dr. John or Junior Mance, Ray Bryant, or Les McCann, *the audience is not going to mind*. If you make a mistake, it is not terribly important to them. They are not deciding whether to sign you to the next record contract or tour. Take a deep breath; remember, your audience is there to have fun, to feel good, not to judge you. When they leave, they will walk away with a good feeling, not a critical account of what you played. Go ahead and release your energy—that is what it is about!

2. Effective Programming

When you sit down to play, you are in complete control of your audience's musical experience. Take that control, but take your time. You don't have to come out with your heaviest guns blazing. Of course, there might be an occasion when you need to impress someone quickly, so judge the situation accordingly. But more often, you can take the time to warm them up. Play a simple introductory chorus or two, perhaps of the left-hand alone. Don't worry about boring them. At the beginning when *their* curiosity is highest, *you* come on modestly, quietly. This gives you time to relax, collect your energies, and build something inside. Let them start to wonder if you have anything to say. Then, when you feel the build-up inside you, let 'em have it! You will be more powerful, and you will grab your listeners at a deeper level. On the other hand, you can open with your strongest tune. Get them on your side; play something you are confident with first, and *then* take some risks.

3. More Advice

There are a number of good books on the psychology of musical performance, which can help you become aware of internal issues that are under your control. Especially recommended is Barry Green's *The Inner Game Of Music* and Stephen Nachmanovitch's *Free Play*.

And above all, have fun!

SUGGESTED READING

METHOD BOOKS

Aebersold, Jamey. *Nothin' but Blues.* (New Albany, IN: Aebersold Publishing, 1971). Excellent play-along booklet and recording, available on cassette or CD.

Baker, David. *Improvisational Patterns: The Blues.* (New York: Charles Colin, 1980). Very complete treatment, including sample choruses, melodic riffs, chord patterns, bass patterns. Contains discography.

Dr. John (Mac Rebennack). *Dr. John the Night Tripper Teaches New Orleans Piano and the Roots of Rock.* (Woodstock, NY: Homespun Tapes, 1985). Five audiocassettes featuring Dr. John talking and demonstrating many aspects of the New Orleans R&B style. Includes cassette of *Dr. John Plays Mac Rebennack.* See also his videos from the same publisher.

Gordon, Andrew D. *100 Ultimate Blues Riffs.* (Ventura, CA: Creative Concepts Publishing Corp., 1995). Comes with either CD or cassette recording or MIDI files on disk. Excellent way to get your creative juices flowing and explore many blues idioms, including R&B, rock, boogie, and gospel.

Gordon, Andrew D. *60 of the Funkiest Keyboard Riffs Known to Mankind.* (Ventura, CA: Creative Concepts Publishing Corp., 1995). Comes with either CD, cassette, or MIDI files. Consisting mostly of two-handed chord accompaniment patterns, this will really help sharpen your rhythmic concept.

Harris, Howard C., Jr. and William B. Fielder. *The Complete Book of Improvisation/Composition and Funk Techniques.* (Houston: DeMos Music Publications, 1980, rpt. 1992). A good introduction to the larger subject of jazz improvisation, this book contains excellent chapters on rhythm, funk grooves, and developing musical ideas.

Harrison, Mark. *The Pop Piano Book.* (Sherman Oaks, CA: Harrison Music Education Systems, 1994). Solid review of pop fundamentals and good accounts of various pop (non-jazz) styles, including pop-rock, R&B, country, and gospel.

Kriss, Eric. *Barrelhouse and Boogie Piano.* (Chester, NY: Music Sales Corp., 1974, rpt. 1994). Instructional guide to these styles with transcriptions of historical recordings.

Kriss, Eric. *Six Blues Roots Pianists.* (Chester, NY: Music Sales Corp., 1973, rpt. 1994). A guide to early blues/boogie-woogie masters, with transcriptions and analyses of their playing.

SEQUENCER/MIDI/COMPUTER PROGRAMS

Blues Pianist, The (Vancouver, BC: PG Music, 1997). Collection of 71 blues performances as MIDI files, appearing on an onscreen keyboard for close study. Henry Butler is one of the featured artists. Also includes biographies and trivia game on blues history. Produced in part by Joel Simpson.

Dick Hyman's Century of Jazz Piano CD-ROM (New Orleans: JSS Music, 1997, 1-800-557-7894). 103 pieces in MIDI files presenting the entire sweep of jazz piano history, with a hefty dose of blues by master multi-stylist Dick Hyman. Includes extensive biographical material, stunning visuals, and rare videos of key figures, including some of the greats of boogie-woogie. Produced by Joel Simpson.

New Orleans Pianist, The (Vancouver, BC: PG Music, 1997). Collection of 65 New Orleans– style performances in MIDI files. In the styles of Professor Longhair, James Booker, Dr. John. Outstanding performers include Henry Butler, Jon Cleary, David Torkanowsky. Produced by Joel Simpson.

MUSIC BOOKS

Boogie-Woogie Beat. (New York: MCA, 1975). 43 piano solo arrangements by various composers, many with lyrics.

Definitive Blues Collection., Ronny Schiff, ed. (Milwaukee, WI: Hal Leonard, 1992). 96 songs of a variety of composers in sheet music form (includes complete piano arrangements).

Handy, W. C., ed. revised by Jerry Silverman. *Blues: An Anthology.* (New York: Collier, 1926, rpt. 1972). Words and music to 53 blues songs (arrangements). Includes a history of the blues by Abbe Niles added in 1949.

Mann, Woody. *The Blues Fakebook.* (New York: Oak Productions, 1995). More than 200 blues tunes in lead sheet form (melody, chords, lyrics). Additional verses are in convenient text form.

Silverman, Jerry. *Folk Blues.* (New York: Macmillan, 1958, rpt. 1968). 110 American folk blues in sheet music form, with a 26-page historical introduction and memos on most of the songs.

BLUES HISTORY

Hannusch, Jeff. *I Hear You Knockin'.* (Ville Platte, LA: Swallow Press, 1985). A history of New Orleans R&B.

Jones, Leroi (Imamu Baraka). *Blues People.* (New York: Morrow, 1963). Jazz and blues in the U.S. as a continuation, transformation, and expression of the African experience.

Larkin, Colin, ed. *The Guinness Encyclopedia of Popular Music.* (Chester, CT: New England Publishing, 1992). In four volumes. A thorough reference of blues artists.

Palmer, Robert. *Deep Blues.* (New York: Penguin, 1981). A musical and cultural history of the Mississippi Delta.

Roberts, John Storm. *Black Music of Two Worlds.* (Tivoli, NY: Original Music, 1972). The survival and transformation of African musical traditions in African-American music.

Small, Christopher. *Music of the Common Tongue: Survival and Celebration in Afro-American Music.* (New York: Riverrun Press; London: John Calder, 1987). Penetrating socio-cultural analysis of music in African societies and its transformation in the New World.

MUSIC PERFORMANCE

Green, Barry with W. Timothy Gallwey. *The Inner Game of Music.* (Garden City, NY: Anchor/ Doubleday, 1986). Excellent analysis and method book on the psychology of performance.

Nachmanovitch, Stephen. *Free Play: The Power of Improvisation in Life and the Arts.* (New York: Putnam, 1990). Provocative philosophical, psychological, and spiritual exploration into the act of improvisation.

PERIODICALS

Blues Revue. Bi-monthly. Subscription office: Rt. 2, Box 118, West Union, WV 26456; Phone: (304) 782-1971. Keep up with the latest in the blues world. Profiles, interviews, ads, classifieds.

Piano Today. Quarterly. Subscription office: P. O. Box 58838, Boulder, CO 80323–8838. Covers classical and jazz piano with some good articles and lessons on blues styles, especially New Orleans styles.

About the Author

Joel Simpson plays and teaches jazz, blues, and popular piano in the New Orleans area. Originally from New Jersey, Simpson earned a Ph.D. from Brown University in Comparative Literature, then moved south to teach English at the University of New Orleans. He left academia to become a performing musician in 1978 and has played around New Orleans and in European festivals since then. In 1994 he earned a Master of Music degree from Loyola University. Since then he has taught jazz and blues piano at Tulane University and in workshops throughout the region.

Simpson has also produced a variety of titles, including the MIDI programs *The New Orleans Pianist, The Gospel Pianist,* and *The Blues Pianist* for PG Music of Victoria, B.C., Canada, and an interactive CD ROM entitled *Dick Hyman's Century of Jazz Piano,* for his own company, JSS Music. This unique product features compositions in the styles of 62 artists, with extensive graphics, videos, and historical backgrounds. In 1994 Simpson's jazz quintet recorded *Subterranean Sweetie,* a CD of originals released on Beat Records. His website is www.jssmusic.com.

Solo Piano Music From CHERRY LANE

The Erroll Garner Songbook, Volume 1

This definitive collection of songs by the legendary jazz pianist and composer includes favorites like "Misty," Dreamy," and "Solitaire." Lavishly illustrated with photos, plus comprehensive performance notes, biography, and discography.

02509912

From "Danny Boy" To "Black Hole Sun"
10 Jazz Arrangements for Solo Piano
by John Colianni

These jazz interpretations of 10 diverse songs are sure to be challenging and entertaining for all pianists! Arranged by jazz piano virtuoso and Concord Jazz recording artist John Colianni, the songs are presented progressively for easy, intermediate or advanced levels, and include performance notes. Features: Danny Boy • Black Hole Sun • Swanee • This Is The Moment • Over There • and more.

02503621

Mark Isham's World

This collection of the jazz and film composer's prolific output includes selections for the film scores *A River Runs Through It*, and *Nell*, as well as his latest jazz (including *Blue Sun*) and children's albums. Biography and photos round out this tribute to one of today's truly exceptional artists.

02503628

Best Of Ragtime Piano
arranged by Max Morath

America's most revered ragtime scholar and performer presents his arrangements of favorite classic piano rags by legendary composers such as Scott Joplin and Joseph Lamb. Includes "The Entertainer."

02503605

Great Riffs Series for Piano

Blues Riffs For Piano
by Ed Baker

The definitive source for blues riffs and licks! Features performance notes for more than 35 audio examples of fills, embellishments, turn-arounds, tags, and licks in the styles of Ray Charles, Dr. John, Professor Longhair, and Johnny Johnson.

02503614 Book/Cassette Pack
02503615 Book/CD Pack

Country Riffs For Piano
by George Wurzbach

The ultimate source for learning country riffs and licks! Features concise performance notes on how to play more than 25 fills, turnarounds, tags, comping patterns, and solos. Also includes a history of the piano in country music, as well as an accompanying audio cassette or CD of the examples, all in one riff-packed, easy-to-follow book.

02503612 Book/Cassette Pack
02503613 Book/CD Pack

Jazz Riffs For Piano
by Frank Feldman

Learn the hottest tags, patterns, turnarounds, and solos in the style of the jazz world's legendary talents, such as Bud Powell, Thelonious Monk, George Shearing, Red Garland, Erroll Garner, Chick Corea, Bill Evans, and Keith Jarrett. Included in this book/audio package are detailed performance notes for all examples.

02503619 Book/Cassette Pack
02503620 Book/CD Pack

Available from Your Local Music Dealer!